MAKE THE CIRCLE BIGGER:

We Need Each Other

MAKE THE CIRCLE BIGGER:

We Need Each Other

Rickie Moore

Humanics New Age, Atlanta, Georgia
Humanics New Age is an imprint of Humanics Limited

Copyright © 1990 by Humanics New Age
Humanics New Age is an imprint of Humanics Limited

All rights reserved.
No part of this book may be reproduced by any means, nor transmitted, nor translated into a machine language, without written permission from Humanics Limited.

First Edition

PRINTED IN THE UNITED STATES OF AMERICA

Library of Congress Cataloging-in-Publication Data

Moore, Rickie.
　Make the circle bigger: we need each other/Rickie Moore.
　　　p. cm.
　Includes bibliographical references (p.)
　ISBN 0-89334-133-9
　1. Group relations training--Cross-cultural studies.
2. Leadership--Cross-cultural studies. I. Title.
HM134.M65　1990
302.3--dc20　　　　　　　　　　90-4065
　　　　　　　　　　　　　　　　CIP

CONTENTS

Acknowledgements vii
Introduction ix

Chapter 1   Harriet Housewife's Survival 1
                  Harriet at a Crossroads 1
                  Harriet in a Group 6
                  Harriet as a Leader 10
                  Harriet's Activities 13
                        No Gossip Rule 13
                        Seven Stretches 13
                        Trance Dance 16
Chapter 2 -   Handsome Harry's Sexuality 19
                  Harry at a Crossroads 19
                  Harry in a Group 23
                  Harry as a Leader 27
                  Harry's Activities 28
                        Gatherings 28
                        Ways 30
Chapter 3 -   Rita Justice's Will Power 33
                  Rita at a Crossroads 33
                  Rita in a Group 38
                  Rita as a Leader 44
                  Rita's Activities 46
                        News and Goods 46
                        Silence 47
                        Support Groups 48
Chapter 4 -   Richard Heart's Love 51
                  Richard at a Crossroads 51
                  Richard in a Group 54
                  Richard as a Leader 59
                  Richard's Activities 62
                        Tri-Energetics 62
Chapter 5 -   Sophia Singer's Communication 65
                  Sophia at a Crossroads 65

	Sophia in a Group	69
	Sophia as a Leader	73
	Sophia's Activities	74
	Sufi Circles	74
Chapter 6 -	Cassandra the Witch's Intuition	79
	Cassandra at a Crossroads	79
	Cassandra in a Group	82
	Cassandra as a Leader	87
	Cassandra's Activities	89
	Ceremonies	89
	Journeys	90
	Chanting	91
Chapter 7	Lucy Leiter's Cosmic Connection	95
	Lucy at a Crossroads	95
	Lucy in a Group	98
	Lucy as a Leader	102
	Lucy's Activities	103
	Messages that Matter	103
The Seven Stretches		104
Bibliography		
	Books that Inspire	111
	Music that Inspires	113
	Organizations that Inspire	114
About the Author		115

ACKNOWLEDGEMENTS

I'm grateful to the playshop family, to the therapists and group leaders in the trainings, and to all members of the human family that care enough to create a future worth preserving, with special thanks to Mikhail Gorbachev, who demonstrates that flexibility, tolerance, and curiosity make the difference between a politician and a great leader. I want to thank Loretta Koopmans for the concept for the cover illustration. Her illustration was born the day the five-billionth person was born on this planet.

    I'm grateful to my soulmate-partner-friend, who speaks the truth and follows his heart. He brings promise for mankind because he knows the strength of his tenderness. A psychologist, he spreads joy with mantras; an expert editor, he transforms run-on ideas into prose; a one-man staff, he turns a bowl of rice into a gourmet feast. During the writing of this book, he gracefully supported me and contributed much. He wrote the mantra section and proved that sooner or later someone's got to punctuate! This book is dedicated to my husband, who knows the power and love and how to use it.

    P.S. The characters in this book are composites of actual people, and therefore cannot be identified with any person, living or dead.

INTRODUCTION

We are all one planet, one race of humans faced with the loss of our life-support systems...our air, food, and water. Nuclear war, environmental pollution, and climatic disasters threaten our very existence.

Much of our personal pain is caused by feelings of helplessness and isolation, and the instinctive yearning to belong and connect with the human family is often lost to loneliness. Gathering in groups is part of the heritage of our endangered species, which may well be one-of-a-kind and worth preserving.

We need each other! As individuals, we need to partake peaceably in the flow of life. As the human family, we are one global being in the process of becoming conscious. Life is an infinite circle, and we have access to its infinite energy when we live with fearless minds and open hearts.

We need to learn how to cooperate, how to organize, how to remain individuals within the context of a group. We need to do more than visualize world peace; we need to realize that peace is personal, profitable, and practical.

If the concept of a peaceful planet seems impossible, how about a world that's more relaxed? If the world is too big to envision, how about starting with your own circle of friends?

Most people are unaware of their capacity for group leadership, yet the world needs good leaders. Look at our leaders and see who our children will follow. A good leader creates changes in communities and campuses, neighborhoods and nations; organizes concerts or conferences, or mother's day out; teaches yoga, kindergarten, or counsels the addicted; leads workshops, or turns a drumming lesson into a therapeutic experience. Group leaders don't need to be therapists, they need to be therapeutic. We humans need all the good leaders we can get, flexible, tolerant, curious people with good intentions who don't control with

Make the Circle Bigger

fear or guilt or empty promises to teach you to walk on water or jump rope without touching the floor.

MAKE THE CIRCLE BIGGER: WE NEED EACH OTHER is written as entertainment, but actually provides methods for enriching relationships between individuals and among members of a group. It is intended to demonstrate how similar human struggles are, and to inspire people to discover their own potential for leadership.

This book describes seven case histories of people from different cultures who discover their hidden talents and untapped power in groups. It is a teaching story, illustrating how people, living in totally diverse situations, on different levels of consciousness, come to a crossroads in their lives, and use the power of the group (and love) to find their way. Each one of the people in this book ultimately becomes a group leader.

Ideally, this book will open your mind and touch your heart; but if it could reach out and take your hand, it would bring you into a circle that you could perhaps lead yourself. This book can show you some ways to do that, motivate you to use your talent for leadership, and show you how you can make the circle bigger.

LEADING A GROUP
A Good Group Leader...

- ▶ Doesn't play follow-the-leader unconciously, but intentionally follows, leads, or changes groups.
- ▶ Knows the value of sitting in circles, because circles end hierarchies and guarantee that nobody is above anyone.
- ▶ Knows the importance of humor, and how to use it.
- ▶ Knows humans are creatures of habit, easily addicted, and thus allows time for people to habituate to new ways of socializing.
- ▶ Knows leaderhsip skills improve with training and experience.
- ▶ Is willing to step into the leader role without ego and without preparation, because as the need arises, the leader appears.
- ▶ Knows when to step out of the role of group leader, and when to ask for help.

Introduction

- Knows to speak little and listen well.
- Is flexible enough to change things she can change, tolerant of what she can't change, and curious to know the difference.
- Never tolerates the intolerable.
- Is spontaneous enough to forego her own agenda in response to the needs of the group.
- IS FLEXIBLE, TOLERANT, and CURIOUS and always respects the NEEDS, WANTS, and INTENTIONS of the members of the group.

If you're a leader willing to take on the unprecedented challenges of today's world crisis, you'll discover your strengths and talents in your own circle. You'll see that there's power in people who work, laugh, scream, and play together; that as a leader YOU can change the course of history and be changed in the process; that every leader lessens the gap between the impossible and the miraculous; and that you belong to a circle that's getting better.

PLAYSHOPS

Inner Peace Playshops are five uninterrupted, inspiring therapeutic days and nights that provide opportunities for groups of twenty to forty individuals to discover the meaning and power of peace. Through personal interaction, music, and heart-opening exercises, participants explore practical methods for coping, for improving personal relationships, and for increasing self-acceptance and esteem. In Playshops we create a compassionate community where we reduce stress and isolation, and rediscover the joy of being human. They provide a safe environment, a sense of belonging and and opportunity for peak experiences, which in themselves awaken higher consiousness and remind us of our potential for greatness. In Playshops people basically get what the whole world wants: friendship, joy, and inner peace.

CHAPTER 1

HARRIET HOUSEWIFE'S SURVIVAL

Harriet was intolerant, inflexible, massively defended, and totally involved with survival issues. When she lost the person she was dependent on for her survival, she realized that she had not developed enough "survival skills" and consequently lost the will to live. She was insecure and self-destructive.

In the loving energy of a supportive group, she was able to accept the truth about herself, and she discovered her own strengths, creativity, intelligence, nurturing instincts, humor, and holiness.

HARRIET AT A CROSSROADS

Nobody knew that Harriet Housewife took seventeen sleeping pills on the morning of her forty-fifth birthday.

She hadn't planned to kill herself, but she awoke from her Valium sleep at 4 a.m., wandered bleary-eyed into the kitchen, sat her two-hundred-pound body at the antique oak table her grandmother had given her, and re-read the letter from Willie.

They'd been married for twenty-four years, she and Willie, and Harriet had it all: a house in Pleasant Villa with enough labor-saving devices to guarantee she would never have to get out of bed, a stack of credit cards, two children (one of each), and a maid every other Thursday.

"Dear Harriet," the letter read like a cross between a nightmare and a bad joke, "We've had some good years, but now I want my freedom."

"Freedom...," Harriet played with the word. "Freedom."

She imagined Willie, his bald head shining, running naked through the neighborhood, flailing his newly-muscled arms and shouting, "I'm free, I'm free!"

"I've hired Dwight Higgens to draw up the divorce. You should be receiving the papers in a few days. Read them carefully and make any changes on a separate piece of paper. Take care of yourself and don't let me down." It was signed, "Bill."

Ever since Willie hired Miss What's-her-name, he insisted on being called Bill. For twenty-four years, really twenty-five, he'd been her Willie. Now, he wouldn't turn around unless you called him Bill. Miss What's-her-name was Janet Ferguson, the secretary Harriet believed was the real reason Willie was divorcing her. Harriet either called her Miss What's-her-name, or Bitch Ferguson.

But if Janet's nickname was "Bitch," Harriet's was "Housewife." She joked about having been born with a gold band on one hand and a toilet brush in the other. She had good naturedly sacrificed enough IQ points to convince herself that it was fulfilling to stay home and cook, clean, and create new and exotic eating disorders.

Willie had always come first. Now she had no husband, the "children" were more grown-up than she. They were away at college, and besides, Mark and Melissa wanted a mother to mother them about as much as she did.

"Shit!" she whispered to herself, "I don't even need a maid every other Thursday."

It was 4:30 a.m. Harriet switched on the giant TV in the kitchen. She saw a cowboy swaggering down the sandy street looking like his pants were full. Harriet laughed until the tears turned sad and wouldn't stop.

"Who am I? Who have I become? What's happened to me? Where's the girl who used to laugh and play and tell jokes and read her kids stories? Where's the Harriet who used to be so sexy her father called her 'Killer Williams, the heart breaker?'"

Oh, how she adored him.

"Daddy!" she screamed, "Why did you have to die so young? Don't be dead, please talk to me, Daddy! Please help me."

"Shit!" she groaned again, "Who can I talk to? Who can I turn to? What's going to become of me? I've had one job in my whole life and..."

She remembered how sweet and supportive Willie had been when after only two days of working as a receptionist in a local beauty salon, the owner returned from vacation, took one look at the flabby, king-sized, uneducated, over-aged woman - and fired her.

"Maybe you can find a better job," Willie had offered, his dark eyes moist.

But Melissa, wearing her mean face, added, "Maybe you'd better take a good look at yourself, Mom."

Harriet tried to stop crying then, but she just couldn't.

She ran into the bathroom, flipped on the light and stared into the mirror.

"Shit!" she said. "I need my glasses."

She rushed back to the kitchen, grabbed her purse, pulled out the glasses and pushed them on her face, running back to the mirror. She began to tremble at her reflection. Harriet had gained a hundred pounds since her wedding. Her once expressive brown eyes were red and swollen, her skin wet and blotchy. Her breasts reached her belly. Two chins hung loosely from her blubbery face.

"I'm old and ugly, constipated and useless," she moaned, "No wonder Willie left. I can't do anything anymore. All I know is how to watch television and shop. I'll bet Bitch Ferguson doesn't even own a TV. I don't even know how to screw anymore, if I ever did in the first place."

She remembered her honeymoon then. She had been so turned-on, so excited, so scared. She was proud to be a virgin for Willie.

And, oh, how she wanted it to be the way she dreamed. She'd cried herself to sleep and made the best of the worst of it for twenty-four years. She secretly believed she was frigid. After all, Willie was perfect.

"There's nobody to cook for in the house, old girl," Harriet was talking to herself, looking into the mirror, tears still streaming. "Nobody to wait up for, nobody to surprise with a frozen fizzy. Nobody even calls me anymore. Help me, somebody, please!" she pleaded.

Then she looked down at the bar of soap sitting innocently in the porcelain dish. "I'm an expert at soaps; I know more about soaps than anybody." She grabbed the bar of soap and automatically sniffed it. "Damn!" she yelled, "I can't even smell anymore," and in a crazy desperation, she stuffed the soap into her mouth. She sank her teeth deep into it and watched herself in the mirror.

"What's become of fat Harriet Housewife?" She moaned and slurped a handful of water and swished it in her mouth. Then, still watching in the mirror, she thought, "Where are my loved ones? Where are my babies? Where's my family?" And she watched the bubbles popping out of her mouth. She coughed, then gasped with horror, watching the soap bubbles spew and splatter the mirror.

"Oh, God!" she sobbed, "Where are my children?" She ached to hold Melissa and Mark. "I need my kids!" she screamed, "I'm scared!"

She realized then that no one had remembered her birthday.

"Willie!" You promised you'd never desert me, you liar! I'm not going to make it, don't you understand? I'm not going to survive this! I need help! Please, somebody help me." And she hung her head over the sink, spitting soap.

It was 5 a.m. Still bending over the sink, resting her huge arms on the basin, a scene floated in her brain. She rinsed her mouth with hot water, then remained still as the pictures became clear and focused.

She saw her favorite TV soap star, Dora Westheimer, lying on a four-poster bed, clad in a white silk robe. Dora was dying. She'd left a memorable note to her adoring public and her lover, and bravely breathed her last into the camera for a heartbroken world of TV devotees.

Death may have been a lousy option for the tired star of "Living Free," but to Harriet it seemed the only way. She opened the medicine chest and there they were: seventeen sleeping pills still left in a bottle.

"I'll write a letter like Dora did," Harriet thought, "I'll make the kids understand. To hell with Willie."

There were no questions, doubts, or hesitations. Pill bottle in hand, Harriet hurried back to the kitchen. She took a pad and pencil from the counter top, sat on her oversized bar stool and wrote:

Dear Melissa and Mark,
I love you with all my heart. I've tried to be a good mother, and although I've made some mistakes, you are both kids I can be proud of. I hope you can forgive me for leaving you, but I know you can take care of yourselves. Please be nice to each

other, don't fight too much, and make sure Dad gives you half of everything he has. You are the greatest gifts life had given me and I will always love you. Please don't hate me. This is the only way.

Mom

P.S. This is my only will. Also, there's $850 in the freezer in a jar labeled "ASPARAGUS."

P.P.S. Give all my clothes to Bitch Ferguson and tell her I hope she grows into them.

Harriet placed the note on the kitchen table, poured a glass of orange juice into a tumbler, and mechanically swallowed the pills.

"I'm going to die doing what I do best," she thought, "I'm going to watch TV." Harriet Housewife walked into her bedroom and donned the only silk outfit she owned. She put on the episode of "Living Free" she'd taped the day before, and lay down to die.

Just as Harriet began to drift away, still awake but not fully conscious, she heard, "Give life a chance." The words floated like musical notes up and down the scale of consciousness. Into the deepest recesses of her drugged and dysfunctional brain, she heard, "Give life a chance, give life a chance."

Stumbling over her own numbed toes, Harriet dragged herself to the toilet. She stuck a couple of fingers down her throat and vomited. She frantically slurped water from the bathroom sink, throwing up again and again.

A song her daughter, Melissa, had written years ago popped into her confused and sleepy brain:

> *Harriet was a housewife*
> *Her life was really plain*
> *Harriet was a housewife*
> *Until she went insane*

Still struggling with her dizziness and blurred visions, and humming the tune to "Harriet Was A Housewife," she successfully brewed a twelve-cup pot of coffee and consumed all but a single cup by 6:15 a.m.

By 7 a.m., she had taken a cold shower, washed her hair, and torn up the letter to her children. She replaced the video cassette with a live broadcast of "Good Morning, World."

By 8 a.m., she was dressed in a grey-flowered muu-muu, had eaten half of a loaf of bread and a bowl of leftover spaghetti, and was walking from room to room trying not to cry. After all, it was her birthday.

HARRIET IN A GROUP

At her daughter's insistence, Harriet went to her first playshop, a five-day one, which was held in a retreat center in the depths of nature. The group room was an enormous converted barn, complete with ancient beams and modern glass walls. A table at the far end of the room was aglow with candles and decorated with flowers. Two huge speakers had been set up, and someone was testing the stereo. The old, wooden floors had been covered with carpet. Colored cushions were laid in a giant circle where some people were sitting meditatively, waiting for things to get started. Others were hugging and greeting people they obviously knew.

Harriet felt totally alone and uncomfortable, despite the smiles and kind words from several people. "I don't belong here! What am I doing?" she thought.

An expectant hush settled over the group as a slender, striking woman walked toward the circle, followed by a slim, bearded man with twinkling eyes. The woman smiled at the assembled faces, her voice brimming with enthusiasm. "I must hug some of the people I know and love! Would you please greet people, especially those you don't know?" Lucy, the group leader, hugged a young woman who ran to greet her.

By the time the group sat in a circle, Harriet felt only a little more stiff and scared than the other first-timers, but she definitely had the most trouble sitting. She hadn't sat on a cushion on the floor for twenty years; she took up two spaces and was painfully aware of it.

Lucy asked people to give their names and briefly state what they needed, wanted, and intended to get from the playshop. If they knew what they wanted to change in their life, they were encouraged to say what that was.

Harriet struggled to get her name out. She couldn't say what she wanted. She didn't know. She did manage to say, "I'm here because my daughter Melissa suggested I come. She thinks I've been...depressed."

The understatement caused a ripple of agreement. Harriet provoked a wide range of responses: pain in some, frustration and even anger in others, but nobody could deny her neediness. She epitomized a woman whose life was not working.

At first, the playshop was hell for Harriet. She considered leaving several times during the first twenty-four hours, and had she not made a commitment to Melissa to stay for all five days, she would have left. By the third day, she'd made great progress.

A NO GOSSIP RULE *(page 13)* gave Harriet a feeling of safety. Lucy made the instructions clear, "The greatest gift we can give each other is the gift of truth. Therefore, if someone does or says something you don't like - tell her. Don't gossip behind anyone's back."

Once Harriet knew that nobody was talking about her, or making fun of her behind her back, she began experiencing herself as an integral part of the familial group energy. She felt accepted. She belonged. She knew people liked her; she could feel it.

She even felt better doing the SEVEN STRETCHES *(page 13)*. The first two days had been ridiculous. She could barely touch her knees when she bent over. Breathing deeply caused her to cough until she choked. Today it was going better.

After the morning's stretches, people were relaxing before breakfast, but Harriet was recuperating. Tall, husky Ron, his head full of auburn hair (kept under control with a brown leather headband), went to give Harriet a hug. He took one look at her weary face and decided to do something nice for her. He reached down like a knight in shining armor, offering her his very muscled arm.

"Please come with me," he smiled warmly.

Without thinking, her huge arms linked with his, Harriet strutted away.

The early morning sun was radiant as Ron led a willing Harriet to an out-of-the-way orchard. He spread a blanket under an old apple tree, took out a bottle of oil from his hip pocket, and motioned for her to lie down, saying, "It's time someone nurtured you without food. I'm going to give you a foot massage." Without waiting for an answer, he knelt at her feet, rubbed the oil into his palms and saturated her feet with it. He held her heels firmly, closed his eyes and breathed.

Ron began massaging Harriet's feet, pressing his fingers deep into her aching soles. She relaxed as he made soothing semi-circles with his knuckles into her instep. He massaged her ankles, rubbed her heels, poked and pushed every joint. He separated her toes and squeezed the tips between his thumb and forefinger with just the right pressure.

It felt great to Harriet, but she was simultaneously worried about her peeling nail polish and felt embarrassed at having anyone touch her fat feet.

When Ron finished, he closed his eyes and sat breathing deeply, lovingly holding her feet in his hands.

Harriet sat up, "Where'd you learn to do that? I'm reborn!"

"Here, yesterday."

Harriet smiled into his face, "The only time anyone ever touched my feet before was when I got a pedicure the day I married Willie."

"Maybe that's why you never knew that your feet are adorable." he said, still holding her feet, "Maybe that's what's wrong with all of us: we have no idea how great we are, because nobody ever tells us."

"What's great about being a housewife?" Harriet prodded.

Ron answered quickly, "Problems exist for all roles, but housewife had taken on a few extra-strength, nausea-inducing aspects."

"Right," Harriet smiled, "the ad for the housewife might read: 'Over-worked slave labor rewarded with disrespect, intolerance, and ingratitude.'"

Ron laughed. "I wouldn't apply for the job. On the other hand, mothering and nurturing are instinctive for some women."

"You mean I did something right playing that role?" Harriet asked.

Ron thought a moment, took her hands in his, looked deep into her eyes, and said, "My mother used to say, 'A housewife is holy when she gives with love.'"

"A holy housewife!" Harriet laughed, thinking, "If Willie could see me now!"

Harriet Housewife's Survival

It was the fourth day. The group had begun a TRANCE DANCE *(page 16)*. Its purpose was to allow people to lose themselves in music and experience their bodies, unencumbered by the usual restrictive movements most of us are taught to do while "dancing."

People were whirling, spinning, jumping, gliding - exploring the freedom to move. They had been asked not to pay attention to each other, rather to keep their eyes unfocused and let the music and sound guide them into a trance.

Harriet loved it. She danced and danced until she felt graceful, fluid, and gorgeous. She swayed herself into an abandon she'd long forgotten.

Suddenly, through half-closed eyes, she unexpectedly caught a glimpse of her reflection in the tall glass doors of the room. She let her Self look, really look, at Harriet Housewife, with an intensity that woke her up. She saw what she had been denying. She saw what she had become.

Lucy saw Harriet beginning to see herself. She watched Harriet, waiting to see what was going to happen. The intensity was so strong as she stood there frozen, staring at her reflection, that soon the whole group was watching Harriet watch herself.

Slowly, purposefully, the group gathered around Harriet, giving her the support she needed to take the first clear look at herself. Everyone knew that she needed to scream, though she struggled against it.

With encouragement Harriet began to take some deep breaths. She inhaled and thought about her Willie, how deeply hurt she was at his abandoning her; she thought about her children, and how hurt she was at their disinterest; she thought about victorious Bitch Ferguson, with Willie to love.

"That's it, breathe! Come on, breathe and let out some sound," Lucy offered, "Let it out or live it out!"

Harriet thought, "I'm a failure, I've wasted my life!" She was shaking. She inhaled with a gasp and stopped thinking. Then, with a wail, she burst into sobs. She grieved for all the years she'd spent asleep, not even dreaming of who she wanted to be. She grieved for all the years she'd stuffed herself full of food to fill her empty soul. She felt her grief and wept. She needed to accept herself as she was, so she could love herself enough to change.

Several people supported her physically so she would not fall to the floor; lovingly they gave her emotional support. They held her huge arms up in the air so she could pull them down and scream.

Harriet inhaled deeply, and people braced themselves against the anger that probably would be released. Again she inhaled...and again...and again...and then, instead of a giant scream, Harriet exploded - with laughter. She laughed a magnificent, radiant, heart-warming laugh that could have cured the world. She laughed at the absurdity of wasting any more time in sadness, anger, and pain. She laughed and laughed and laughed.

A jovial celebration erupted, full of playful, loving hugs and kisses. A new-born Harriet was seated in the center while the exhilarated group sang "Happy Birthday," and a woman who had never really known herself realized just how lovable she was. Harriet had decided to LIVE!

HARRIET AS A LEADER

One year and several playshops later, in her newly converted living room, a slim and healthy Harriet was teaching the SEVEN STRETCHES *(page 13)* to a group of fat women who were determined to lose weight. She was standing with her beautiful, well-toned arms up above her head, explaining the first position to the group when without warning, she laughed out loud and said, "I know about being fat, ladies, because until recently, I was a morbidly obese woman who believed her place was underneath her husband."

The women stretched their arms to the sky and laughed with her.

"I was born believing a woman can't survive without a man, and that men are the holier, more valuable of the species. Now I know what it is to be a holy housewife. Keep stretching," she encouraged, as they struggled to keep their arms up, "I discovered that dead food and an empty heart make us fat."

Now they were in the second position, bending over with their hands touching the floor, struggling to keep their legs straight. "I learned to use my survival skills to make life an adventure, and you can, too. But remember," Harriet said, still bending over,

"We can only use what we have learned to use."

She began telling the truth to these women who desperately needed to learn how to make real changes in their bodies and in their lives, and they were so enthralled by listening to her, they forgot how difficult it was to hold the stretches.

"Last year," Harriet went on, "I began to videotape myself losing weight. Keep breathing," she encouraged, "I am going to show you the cassettes after we finish our session today."

Then Harriet led them into the third position. They were standing, arched back into graceful bows.

"I discovered the value of live foods, like fruits and vegetables; but most of all, I found how empty most of us are in our hearts and souls, and I discovered the value of soul food."

The women were smiling, straining, and fascinated.

"You're doing great," she said enthusiastically, "Keep breathing. The point is, we can't discover anything if we're drugged out. Most Americans are addicts - hooked on six or seven hours of hardcore television just to fall asleep. We need to stay asleep because what we see when we wake up is too painful to watch."

They were in the fourth stretch. Some of the women couldn't get into the position at all, but Harriet began helping those who were having the most difficulty.

"That's it. You can do it," she helped one particularly queen-sized, out-of-shape woman who was practically in tears, "I couldn't touch my knees when I started to go though rebirth at mid-life. I had no idea how important flexibility was. I was lonely and so intolerant, my only friends were my children and they couldn't stand me. Keep up. Keep breathing. I met a man at Overeaters Anonymous who fell in love with me and offered to let me cook for him, do his laundry, and wash his car - if I was a good woman and kept him satisfied sexually, of course."

Some of the women groaned, and others laughed, but they kept on stretching.

Now they were in the fifth position. For many of the women it was painful, but Harriet kept on motivating them.

"I had so little self-respect, I thought I was lucky to receive his offer."

More laughter.

"My daughter and my son came to visit me after I'd lost about sixty pounds, and after they recovered from the shock of seeing me look like a normal person, I read them a poem I'd written. Keep stretching and I'll recite it for you now:

> *On Monday I'm strong*
> *By Tuesday I'm weak*
> *Wednesday, optimistic*
> *On Thursday it's bleak*
> *Friday goes great*
> *Saturday I cry*
> *Sunday I'm joyous*
> *Monday I could die*
> *In the morning I'm up*
> *By afternoon, down*
> *Spend the evening a guru*
> *Wake up like a clown!*

"Change hands," Harriet said calmly. And the women, half-hypnotized, changed hands and kept stretching.

"I sold the still pictures from my weight-loss video to a magazine, and realized I could be independent. I earned a reputation as a peer counselor for weight reduction, fitness, and health because after all, who understands over-eaters better than a junk food junkie? That's it. Now put both hands in front of you. You're almost there. Breathe. You can change your life, too."

> *You need to live NOW*
> *Not remember back when*
> *You can live happily*
> *As a size ten*

Everyone laughed.

"Now, inhale deeply, and come up as gracefully as you can."

Harriet watched as fifteen fat women stood silent and serene, then lay down on the carpeted floor for a much deserved rest.

"Now," Harriet whispered loudly, "relax deeply. And as you breathe into your heart center, visualize yourself as a beautiful, strong, slim, healthy goddess whose life can be filled with love. You can metamorphose from a caterpillar to a butterfly if you open your hearts and let yourself feel a little compassion for yourself. Please be good to you and forgive yourself your mistakes. You are human. Whether eighteen or eighty, you are a child of the universe, and you deserve to be loved."

And suddenly Harriet realized she had just witnessed a miracle. Everyone had done their stretches; they had made it, with a little help from HER.

HARRIET'S ACTIVITIES
No Gossip Rule

It is normal for people to criticize and judge each other. Therefore, establishing a No Gossip Rule can offer a sense of safety and trust. It's a good idea to establish a No Gossip Rule in any ongoing group, and it's important to reiterate the rule because bad habits are hard to break.

Not gossiping doesn't mean not talking about other group members. Active interest in members of one's group is important and rewarding. The rule simply means that criticizing someone's behavior without telling the person directly does no one any good. If you want to help someone, tell them directly with kindness and love.

Seven Stretches

Once there was a shaman who fell three stories and broke all the bones in his body. Instead of dying, he learned many secrets of life. Among them was the secret of keeping the body flexible through a quickly addictive series of stretches. These stretches have proven to be a remarkably reliable way to maintain the strength of the muscles and the alignment and flexibility of the spine, thus stabilizing the nervous system, regulating the hormones, and quieting the mind. Moreover, they require a minimum of time (five to seven minutes will do), although the longer each position is held, the greater the results. The stretches are simple - not easy. Like all exercises, they can be done alone, but they are noticeably easier when done in a group (don't believe me, try them yourself).

To begin, being barefoot is best. Be sure your clothes are loose and comfortable. Shake the body a little, consciously bringing your attention and awareness to yourself. Be in the moment. Remember, this is your time. These few minutes belong to you. You have no one else to worry about, and nothing in the world is more important than taking care of yourself. Giving to yourself is the first necessary step that enables you to give to anyone else.

1ST STRETCH. This position can be held for as little as two or three deep breaths, or as long as it feels comfortable or needed. Stand with the feet underneath the shoulders, toes pointing straight ahead. Inhale deeply through the nose and exhale through the mouth. After a few breaths, slowly raise both arms in the air and reach for the sky. Hands are separated shoulder-width apart. Bring both arms close to the ears and parallel to each other and stretch for all you're worth, inhaling through the nose and exhaling through the mouth.

Transition. Inhale deeply, and with the exhale slowly bring the hands to the floor, bending from the hips with the back as straight as possible. Bend the knees as much as needed to allow the palms to rest flat on the floor, the heels of the hands a few centimeters in front of the tips of the toes, fingers facing forward.

2ND STRETCH. Hold for a minimum of one minute. Inhaling through the nose and exhaling through the mouth, begin to push the palms against the floor and slowly raise the hips toward the sky. Focusing on the hips raising toward the sky enables you to stretch the hamstrings more easily. This way the legs become straight faster. Relax the head, let it fall, and enjoy yourself.

Transition. Inhale long and deep, slowly straightening the spine, uncurling vertebra by vertebra. With feet still directly under the shoulders, bend backwards in a bow with the hands tucked behind you in the crease between the buttocks and the thigh. Keep the thumb connected to the index fingers; don't separate the thumb from the rest of the hand.

3RD STRETCH. Stand with the knees bent slightly, feet directly under the shoulders, toes pointing straight ahead, and thumbs pushed into the crease of the buttocks. Bend backwards and look up at the sky. Pull the shoulders back and push the heart center forward. The position should look like one continuous graceful curve from the feet to the top of the head. This is not a difficult stress position; relax into it.

Transition. Exhale forward out of the posture, and gracefully sink to the knees, positioning them shoulder-width apart.

4TH STRETCH. Take hold of the heels (right hand on right heel, left hand on left heel), inhale, and stretch the belly toward the sky, letting the head fall behind you. The arms are completely straight, with elbows locked. This posture is difficult for most of us, but with practice and perseverance it becomes easier. The deeper you breathe, the easier it becomes.

Transition. Inhale, then exhale yourself slowly forward and place both hands in front of you, with palms resting on the floor, fingers pointing forward. Knees are still under the shoulders. Relax the spine. Spread the feet out as far as they comfortably go without moving the knees. Push the hands against the floor, straighten the toes so they're pointing forward, and raise the hips toward the sky until the legs are straight. Feet are approximately one meter apart, and hands are approximately one meter in front. With the buttocks in the air, you look like a perfect triangular pyramid.

5TH STRETCH. Keeping the right hand in place, put the left hand under the heel of the left foot (reach around the outside of the left foot), stepping gently on the fingers of the left hand. This activates the reflex points in the fingers of the left hand. Relax the head against the right arm, and be sure the feet and right hand are equal distance apart.

Transition. Switch hands.

6TH STRETCH. The same as the fifth, but with the left hand in front, and the right hand under the right heel.

Transition. Put the right hand next to the left.

7TH STRETCH. Both hands one meter in front, feet one meter apart, bring the buttocks as high up to the sky as possible. Keep the arms straight and relax the head against them, so that you are a perfect triangular pyramid. Enjoy yourself.

Transition. Slowly walk the feet together until they are shoulder-width apart, and walk the hands back toward the feet. Slowly straighten the spine, inhaling up until you are standing straight. Take a breath and experience what you have done for yourself. At this point the needs of each of us, the subtleties and refinements, vary from individual to individual. It is good to take a few minutes to rest, either standing or lying on your back.

Note (1). CHANTING (*p. 91*) can be an easy way to know how much time is spent in each position.

        ONG NAMO GURU DEV NAMO
        ONG NAMO GURU DEV NAMO
        NAMO NAMO GURU DEV NAMO
        NAMO NAMO GURU DEV NAMO

This chant takes one full minute as each line is sung on a deep breath. It calls upon the inner teacher and helps to heal emotions and awaken the spirit.

Note (2). Some people prefer to inhale through the nose and exhale in long full sounds. This releases tensions and often causes spontaneous healing laughter.

Note (3). Other prefer inhaling through the nose and blowing the air out the mouth with a whooshing sound.

The remarkable power of these stretches becomes more and more clear as the author receives feedback from people who do them. They satisfy the need for developing and maintaining flexibility in a minimum of time. As distasteful as quick cure and fast food syndromes can be, the reality is that most of us do not have ample time for the care and maintenance of our bodies. My gratitude to Adano Ley (1987) runs deep.

Trance Dance

When dancers become one with the rhythm of life and flow with it, dancing becomes meditation, and it heals the soma, psyche, and spirit.

Although it is certainly possible to enjoy dancing alone, dancing in a group without worrying about learned "steps" or thinking about how you're "supposed" to look can clear the mind and energize the body.

Invite a few friends to get together for an evening of Trance Dance. Clear an ordinary living area of furniture (or rent an easily accessible room for an evening). Play appropriate rhythmic music and let the person acting as group leader instruct people to keep their eyes only half opened and flow and go until you become one with the music *(Ley, 1987)*. Let the body move itself. Let the inspiration inside you guide the moves, and enjoy a natural state of altered consciousness.

It's always best after a shared activity to come together in a circle to share individual experiences, or enjoy a moment of silence together.

P.S. Avoid smoky rooms, fluorescent lights, high prices, and low lyrics. Much of what we listen to and absorb into our unconscious comes from the messages of modern music *(Hamel, 1976)*. Be cautious when listening to words that support unwanted habits. High-conciousness music is beautiful, uplifting, and healing *(Freedman, 1987)*. Make conscious choices and be clear about your intention.

CHAPTER 2

HANDSOME HARRY'S SEXUALITY

Harry's sexuality dominated his life. Driven by lust, he suffered low back pain and compulsive behavior. Abandoned in his youth through his mother's death, he was afraid of intimacy, of loving totally, and consequently was attracted to women he didn't know, often remaining impotent with his wife. Harry learned to open his heart and transform his potent sexual energy into a sacred bond of love and trust between himself and his wife. Together they changed stifling social obligations, commonly called "parties," into Gatherings where people could explore new and healthier Ways of relating.

HARRY AT A CROSSROADS

Handsom Harry was the type of guy who would regularly walk into a room, notice a good-looking woman, catch her eye, stare with enormous intensity, and go into his routine: "This is IT! I'm falling in love! You're the ONE!"

Despite his head full of silky waves of black hair, startling blue eyes, and perfect body, Harry seemed doomed to forever search for the perfect partner - until he met Anna, an ordinary woman with a whipped-puppy look and cocker spaniel eyes.

After her first look at Harry the Magnificent, Anna was convinced that if she couldn't have him she'd either join a convent or the Salvation Army. Her beautiful sister, Elke, was attracted to Harry, too, but Harry found Anna's adoration for him irresistible, and he married her.

Seven years later, Harry was running a successful restaurant, and his lust was running him. Not every woman he saw became an object of his fantasy, only those he liked. As his interest in other women waxed, his interest in Anna waned.

Anna was a patient woman. Plain women often are. But even patient women need love.

Make the Circle Bigger

Harry had a problem. Strangers, women he didn't know, to whom he had no obligations, turned him on. He found the intrigue of a "stolen cookie" or a "roll in the hay" with a sexy woman irresistible. On the other hand, though he loved Anna, she was his "wife," and Harry found the role annoying. Besides, whenever he opened his heart and felt a loving glow, he got a cold chill and lost his erection.

One sultry summer day, in the midst of Harry and Anna's long cold war, Elke stopped by the restaurant, offering Harry a warm hug and a good look at her breasts. He went home early that night, determined to rekindle some romance with his "wife." Fortunately, he found Anna receptive.

The evening went well. The more relaxed Harry became, the more turned-on he felt.

After a candlelight dinner, Anna prepared a bubbly bath, and they splashed and played like children, trying to recapture the fun and the joy they had once shared.

After Harry drank a lot of wine, he began to feast his eyes on Anna. She was sitting across the tub, wet and wonderful. He drank in the beauty of her form (even wives can have great breasts). He reached for her, and inhaled the fragrance of her body. His blood raced.

"Would you like some more wine?" Anna asked coyly.

No response.

"Something else?"

He smiled.

"Anything?"

His response was a kiss. He began exploring her mouth with his tongue. Slowly, they stood, and silently and tenderly dried each other. He kissed her eyelids, her nose, and ears. He licked her lips with his own and with his mouth still covering hers, he guided her to bed and placed her on the fresh white sheets.

"Harry. . ." she whispered.

"Shhh. No more words," he instructed.

She sighed deeply, relaxed, surrendering.

Excitement streamed through his body, throbbed between his legs. He climbed up onto the bed, lay next to her, reached for her breast and moaned, "Oh, ...Elke!"

Harry tried to choke on the word, but it was too late. Anna

froze. He tried to speak, instead he stuttered, "I...I...I'm sorry, Anna. I don't know why I...I...I..."

"I...I...I know why you said 'Elke'," Anna mimicked him, "You said 'Elke' because you were wishing you were with Elke and not me." And Anna began to cry.

"Look, she just came into my mind at that moment, but there's nothing between Elke and me." Harry bit his lip remembering how turned-on he had been to Elke just hours before, and the night he and Elke really had quite a time together (but he had totally discounted the experience because they both had had too much to drink). Harry added, "Maybe I do fantasize about her from time to time. What's wrong with fantasizing about other women?" he asked, immediately wishing he hadn't.

"ELKE IS MY SISTER, YOU ASSHOLE!" Anna screamed, hitting him in the face with her pillow.

"Okay, you're right. That is a stupid thing to do, even though she is sexy."

"SHE'S sexy?! SHE'S sexy?! What am I? A frigid, undersexed idiot?"

"Well, we haven't exactly been turning each other on lately, and ..."

"And I suppose that's my fault? It's MY fault that we're not making love. Is it my fault that you're disinterested and preoccupied? My fault that you don't have as much patience or desire for me as you do for your restaurant or anyone who wiggles by? It's NOT MY FAULT that you can't control your..."

Harry interrupted and said mechanically, "There you go again. Don't think your nagging doesn't drive me away from you." He scrambled out of bed, and reaching for his underwear, added, "In fact, nagging is not at all sexy."

"Very funny," Anna said, unimpressed, "But the deadline for complaints was yesterday."

"Besides," Harry said, trying to smile, "I didn't say it was all your fault."

"That's big of you! You're really growing."

"So what do you want me to do? I'm the same guy you married. I haven't changed. Now, that's not good enough for you. Well, if you want to make an enemy of someone, try to change him."

Make the Circle Bigger

Anna got out of the bed and walked straight to Harry. Her open face was as naked as she was. "I want you to be more sensitive to me, more patient. I want you to...to be a lover to me."

Harry got defensive and turned away, "Most couples taper off with time. I know we don't screw like we used to."

Anna winced, "That's just it, Harry! That's the point: you don't make love, you screw. Besides, not all couples lose interest in each other. There are ways to increase sexual pleasure, with practice."

Harry laughed good-naturedly, "Use it or lose it! And when did you become an expert on sexology? Who've you been screwing that you want to give me lessons?"

Anna didn't bite. "I want us to be who we said we were to each other when we got married. I want you to be my partner. I want you to be as turned-on to me as you are to strangers."

Harry was stunned, knowing it was true. "You really do look great when you're mad." He tried reaching for her.

"You can't sweet-talk your way out of this, Harry. I've had it! This is it. Either we both do something to make this marriage work, or I'm leaving you!"

Harry was stunned again, and hurt. Never in their seven years together had Harry ever once considered, at least not consciously, that Anna might leave him. She was a fixed asset, a permanent fixture. It was Plain Anna who should worry about being left - Plain Anna, not Handsome Harry.

He asked, "What do you want from me? I work hard. I've never hit you..."

Anna pulled back. "You hit me every time you flirt with someone in public or screw someone in private! Every time you embarrass me, you're being violent."

"Jesus! Now what? When did I embarrass you?" Harry got up and walked to the other side of the room.

"Oh, for heaven's sake, stop it! Open your eyes. Everyone knows how you are. You're almost a joke. People call you Horny Harry. While you right eye's watching a pair of breasts, your left eye's on somebody's ass."

"That's how I AM. I like women. I like sex. I refuse to dry up. I like myself the way I am. I refuse to change." He stood defiant, staring at Anna. "Take it or leave it!"

"Harry," she said absolutely, "I'm not going to take it!"

HARRY IN A GROUP

Harry and Anna sat next to each other in the opening circle of a playshop. The room glowing in the candlelight was far more beautiful than Harry had anticipated. So were the people. He hadn't known what to expect, but he was delighted with what he saw.

Lucy asked people to state why they were there.

Harry said brightly, "I'm here because my wife said if I didn't come to this playshop with her, she would leave me," and everyone laughed, especially Anna.

After brief introductions, the group began to experience different WAYS (p. 30) of getting to know each other and themselves better. Sitting in front of someone he'd never met before, Harry was to tell one of the worst experiences of his life. Three minutes later, in front of another stranger, he described the roles he had played. In three minutes, with another person, he had to talk nonstop, telling his partner all the reasons why he was lovable.

After he'd heard and shared a significant number of important life issues, Harry realized how similar most people's problems were, and he quickly lost his nervousness. He began to enjoy himself.

During one exercise, Harry sat across from a distinguished looking grey-haired man. Using only facial expressions, hand motions, and sound, they were to tell each other all their complaints about life, without words. Harry watched the man gyrating his tongue, flailing his fingers, rolling his eyes, grunting, groaning, screeching and clearing his throat, as he explained his life without words. Amazingly, he understood the guy. And even more terrific for Harry, when it was his turn, the man understood him.

Harry was surprised at how much he liked sitting on the floor interacting with a group of people truthfully. He was relieved not to be playing the macho man, and happy not to be wearing his same old mask.

Next, Harry was sitting opposite an attractive young woman with enormous wise eyes.

The instructions to the group were: "Let yourself look at this person. Really SEE. Look at the shape of the face, notice whether one eye is larger than the other, notice the color of the eyes. It's not who you know, but HOW you know who you know."

Harry began to feel a little uneasy. He was unaccustomed to looking deep into anyone's eyes, even Anna's, without being sexy.

The instructions continued, "This is not a man, woman, or child in front of you. This is a human being. Now close your eyes and let yourself see this person as a young child. See the child acting role. ALL CHILDREN PLAY ROLES IN ORDER TO SURVIVE. Feel what the child needs, wants. Take your time, and when you're ready, slowly open your eyes, and share what you've seen with your partner. Don't be afraid to be wrong. Just tell your partner what you saw.

Harry surprised himself. He had always been more skeptical than curious about intuition. Especially his own. But he saw her clearly. She was sitting in a small dreary kitchen looking frail and afraid. There was no one else in the scene. She simply sat, looking pitiful.

Harry opened his eyes, and saw the same attractive woman in a totally different light. He told her compassionately what he had seen.

"That's amazing," she said enthusiastically, "I spent half of my childhood alone in the kitchen."

Harry was having a good time now.

Then it was her turn. She looked at him, and as she closed her eyes, Harry could almost feel her taking in a total picture of himself. After a few minutes, his partner shared, "I saw you walking barefoot into your mother's bedroom, a little teddy bear stuffed under your arm, rubbing your eyes with the back of your hand. You pulled the covers back from her high bed, and I saw your intense sadness when you realized the bed was empty. Then I saw you acting the role of a cocky kid who didn't give a damn about anything, especially his mother."

Harry's mother had slept in a high four poster bed, had indeed died when he was six, and he still owned the teddy bear.

By the end of the third exercise, Harry had gained a whole new respect for psychic abilities, especially his own.

He was comforted by being among people who were willing to take a look at their own lives long enough to make them better.

By the end of the first night, Harry and Anna had made a

startling discovery: they both wanted their marriage to work.

The next day Harry was behaving strangely, for Harry. He was able to look people in the eye, and he had become curious about people. He discovered that when he got interested in other people's problems, it gave him some relief from his own.

On the fourth day, there was a men's group and a women's group. Intimate sharing with a group of men was one more experience Harry had never had. The men's group accelerated in intensity until all the men were finally able to express their rage in some wonderful, wild screams.

By the end of the group, Harry felt great. He lay on his back with a smile from ear to ear. He was calmer than he every remembered. He thought, "One good scream's worth a thousand words."

Just as Harry's eyes were about to close, as the feeling of peace was settling in, he heard Anna crying. He let her cries come into his ears, and he took responsibility for every one of them. He felt guilty. The guiltier he felt, the angrier he became. He stood up and the next thing he knew, Lucy encouraged him to sit opposite Anna on a mattress.

"What are you crying about?" Lucy asked Anna.

"I'm crying because I'm so damn happy that Harry's here letting it out."

"Why else?"

"I'm crying..." Anna wiped her eyes with the back of her hand, "because it's sad to love someone who's afraid to love."

Lucy said, "Harry, please look into Anna's eyes and complete the sentence I give you without thinking. And Anna, please repeat back only what Harry says. Harry, you're to continue repeating the same sentence and finishing it until your time is up, about two minutes. Okay, 'What I like about you is...'"

Harry said, "What I like about you is the way you're taking responsibility for yourself in this playshop."

Anna smiled, "What you like about me is the way I'm taking responsibility for myself in this playshop."

Harry said, "What I like about you is your smile."

"What you like about me is my smile," Anna said, smiling wider.

"What I like about you is the way you stand by me even when I act like a jerk."

Make the Circle Bigger

"What you like about me," Anna started, but tears came to her eyes, and she had a hard time finishing the sentence.

Harry tenderly wiped the tears from Anna's eyes, and she cried some more.

Harry went on, "What I like about you is the way you want me."

"What you like about me is the way I want you," Anna said, still crying, but happy.

And the sentences changed to, "What I want from you is..."

"What I want from you is less nagging," Harry stared at her.

"What you want from me is less nagging."

"What I want from you is help," Harry caught his breath and listened.

Anna repeated, "What you want from me is help."

She had been feeling resentful, bitter, hurt, and had been nagging him. But now she felt powerful, needed, and forgiving.

When it was Anna's turn, the first sentence was, "Everything would be fine with us if only you would..."

Without thinking she said, "Everything thing would be fine with us if you would stop chasing other women."

"Everything would be fine with us if I would stop chasing other women," Harry said, as pictures of himself doing his routine flashed on the motion picture screen in his head. He got the picture. He didn't like the role anymore. But even more, he didn't like what it was doing to Anna.

Once Anna said, "Everything would be fine with us if you would see me for who I am, not as your mother."

Harry heard her. A tear slipped from his eye and, perhaps for the first time, Harry saw Anna. She wasn't plain either, she was exquisite. He saw her sweet, soft, reddened face wet with tears. He saw HER, not a mother, not a wife, but a woman, a beautiful woman who really loved him.

Anna said, "Everything would be fine with us if you would want me again." And a tear trickled down her cheek.

"Everything would be fine with us if I would want..." and Harry began to cry, "I do want you! Oh, God, I love you so much..." He reached out and took her in his arms. He squeezed her close and she hugged him tight. He held her and they both cried.

"I love you," he kept repeating, "I love you." He held her as his heart pounded and pumped the blood through his veins, "I love you." He kissed her face, her eyes, her hands, her hair, "I love you," and only Anna knew he had an erection.

HARRY AS A LEADER

Two years and four playshops later, Harry and Anna began turning ordinary parties into GATHERINGS *(p. 28)* for fun and self-knowing.

Their group leading began innocently, when they decided to celebrate their eighth anniversary. They were happy, loving, and turned-on to each other, and they wanted their friends and family to share their joy.

What they didn't want was an ordinary party where people felt isolated, played stupid roles, tried to impress each other, spilled drinks, flirted when they shouldn't, fidgeted and left early, or stayed too late because they drank too much.

Harry and Anna wanted to interact with their friends in a new and meaningful way.

Harry suggested they make a circle and everyone give an imaginary gift to someone there. "You can give a gift of heart," he said enthusiastically, "You can give anybody anything! From a new self-image, to a holiday in the South Seas! Give verbal gifts to each other, not just to Anna and me."

At first people offered ridiculous comic gifts, but before long it became an opportunity for people to give openly and honestly, something of meaning. And it was fun.

When it was his turn, Harry gave Anna a promise: "I commit to becoming a masterful, monogamous lover. I release you from the role of wife, and offer you the role of goddess."

Anna blushed and everyone cheered, even Elke, who looked at Harry with respect, and without making sexy overtures.

Then Harry and Anna announced that they wanted to play out, just for fun, the changes they had made in their marriage.

A few pillows were tossed in the middle of the living room, and it was instantly converted into a theater. They began acting out a scene from their life together. They portrayed themselves in the roles they had been playing before making a real commitment to each other: the disinterested husband comes home to the nagging wife.

After a standing ovation and thundering applause, as an encore, Harry and Anna played themselves in their new roles as beloved life partners. This time, they were adorably sexy and loving and interested in each other's words and facial expressions. Anna, acting like a luscious goddess in the tantric tradition, looked into Harry's eyes and over-dramatically, theatrically played, "I intend to turn our sexual energy and our relationship into a vehicle for reaching the ultimate ecstasy."

Instead of reacting with the same playful humor, Harry took her hands, his eyes sparkling with sincerity, and said seriously, "I intend to learn all I can about love, about loving, and lovemaking, because I know I can only use what I've learned to use, and I want to be all I can be - for you."

Anna beamed and everyone cheered.

"I think that ever since you've opened your heart," Anna said, "you've become totally irresistible," and she whispered in his ear, "and I know you have an erection!"

HARRY'S ACTIVITIES
Gatherings

We all need to belong. Nothing cures loneliness like being connected with other people of like mind and heart, people with similar needs, wants, and intentions.

In these difficult times, it is especially important to feel a real and meaningful connection with our sister/brother travelers on this great, endangered planet.

People like to "party." But the term has often become synonymous with low consciousness, drug- and alcohol-induced gossipy, boring, unrewarding frivolity.

There are alternatives! If you can get clear on your own intentions, you can transform low consciousness parties into gratifying experiences. We need each other! And there are many ways of celebrating our interdependence.

Simply get a group together, make a CIRCLE, and take turns sharing what's going on in your lives. When people sit in a circle, they immediately abolish a hierarchy; no one is more important than anyone else.

This is a good time to use a TALKING STICK, or any object to which you assign power. If you don't have a formal Talking Stick, you could use a rock, a flower, etc. People are more conscious of what they are saying when the only time they can talk is when they are holding the power object. When people speak one at a time, everyone tends to pay more attention to what they say. With normal party chatter, people either try to impress, seduce, or defend themselves. When people speak one at a time, the level of consciousness is always raised, and so is the level of curiosity. The more curious we are, the less defensive we become.

Invoke a NO GOSSIP RULE *(p.13)* and raise your consciousness automatically. If you can't say something nasty or critical about someone, you'll have to talk about something important. Become creative, curious, and free from the normal social games that keep us defended and scared.

REWRITE THE LYRICS TO A FAMOUS SONG. For example this can be sung to the tune of "Silent Night."

> *Silent Me, Holy Me,*
> *I am calm, I am Free.*
> *'Round me beams a bright white light,*
> *Keeping me safe both day and night.*
> *Goddess and I are one...*
> *God and I are one.*

A few people planned a gathering with the theme: "New Men, New Women". After sharing their views and enjoying a great debate, the group spontaneously wrote lyrics to "Battle Hymn of the Republic" in honor of new women and men. *(Rowan, 1987)*

Here is "Goddess Dance."

Mine eyes have seen the glory of the waking of women.
They are strong and independent and they won't be ruled by men.
They trust their intuition and their power's been released,
And they'll lead us into peace.
Glory, glory, times are changing,
Glory, glory, times are changing,
Glory, glory, times are changing,
And the goddess dances on.

*Mine eyes have seen the glory of the coming of new men,
They are flexible and tolerant and they understand women.
They're more curious and loving than they've ever been before,
And they'd rather make love than war.
Glory, glory, times are changing,
Glory, glory, times are changing.
Glory, glory, times are changing,
And the goddess dances on.*

SURVIVAL PARTIES are groups of people gathered together to help each other through specific, life-threatening situations. For example, a corporation sought a permit to inject unstable underground salt domes with highly toxic materials that threatened a community's water supply. Residents held a survival party, raised enough funds to stop the project, and then had a giant celebration.

CELEBRATIONS, unlike protests, connect people in a positive, optimistic attitude and can be help for anything from someone's un-birthday to "let's celebrate that we still have safe water."

For example, a few hundred people gathered in a major city to celebrate the cancellation of a proposed nuclear power plant. This celebration united the residents.

FULL MOON GATHERINGS. The moon gets full every month. It's one of the few things you can count on. People all over the planet gather to watch the same moon and stars. They celebrate, make new friends, and stay in touch with nature's cycles and with the people they love.

When the world is in crisis, it's wise to celebrate our universal struggle for survival, and it's intelligent to use our time creatively. So the next time you're invited to a "party", you might ask, what's the intention?

Ways

These WAYS of getting to know people *(and yourself)* better are generally done sitting in a circle, with people facing a partner, making eye contact. The group leader explains what to do and how long to take. A time limit is always given, and so is a reminder when time is up.

1. Sit across from a partner. Look at each other. Take a breath

and relax. The person who is going to go first, raise your hand (it's interesting to note that one of the two partners invariably raises his or her hand first). Now, the person who goes first, please relax, because your job is to listen. For the next three minutes, you will listen to your partner without interrupting. If you're going to speak, please tell your partner everything about your past, non-stop, for three minutes. Tell how you were brought up, what your past was like, BUT do not say one word of truth! LIE! For three straight, uninterrupted minutes, LIE. Be creative, inventive, have fun. Lie.

2. Sitting across from a partner, please tell each other the worst episode of your life, only this time when you repeat what happened, tell it like a comedy. Make it as absurd, as funny as you can. Take turns.

3. Look at your partner. See who she or he reminds you of. Now tell each other about the person each of you remind the other of. Share fully.

4. Looking at your partner, tell about your future plans. Be as unrealistic as you choose, but be creative about your future visions.

5. Explain to your partner what happened when some significant person in your life was inflexible, intolerant, and defensive with you. Give details about the incident, and how you were hurt by it. Switch after you've either cried, or laughed enough.

6. Sitting across from a partner tell each other about your first experience with the opposite sex, or your last.

7. During playshops, people learn to respect each other for no reason at all. Once we get over our fears and basic insecurities about ourselves, we're usually tolerant and loving. An interesting and intense way of getting to know another person is to ask, "What do you need? What do you want? What do you intend?" The partner asking the questions changes intonation and intuitively alternates the questions. The one answering says the first thing that comes to mind.

8. With the group seated, facing the center, the leader can go around the circle letting people complete sentences. The instructions are to repeat the phrase and complete it without thinking. The experience becomes more intense if the leader alternates who begins the round of sentence completion. Some ideas for

sentences are:

- *My mother always...*
- *When I was a child, I felt...*
- *I'm most afraid of...*
- *Being a man means...*
- *The ideal partner is...*
- *Right now I need (want, intend)...*

CHAPTER 3

RITA JUSTICE'S WILL POWER

Rita was angry, addicted to nicotine, needing to separate from her mother, and fighting for her individuality. She was torn between her need for freedom and her need for love. Her successful social role was an empty reward, a substitute and excuse for what was otherwise an unsatisfying lifestyle. When she experienced Silence in a supportive group, she broke out of her roles, made peace with her mother, and converted her strong will power into a noble intention. Rita rallied Support Groups, organized for political justice, and inspired people to take a stand. She led groups as a speaker and by her example.

RITA AT A CROSSROADS

It was 2 p.m. when attorney Rita Justice walked into her mother's canary-yellow papered kitchen. With her mane of auburn hair neatly coiled around the top of her head and her brown eyes sparkling, Rita epitomized success. She only hoped her mother would notice. After all, Frances Flunk was nearly deaf, but she could still see.

Rita had worked hard for the respect she was getting in the legal community. She had struggled to get through law school, a divorce, and a preganacy, all without any help from her ex-husband. Now, Rita was living happily with a man she loved, her son Steven was married and about to become a father, and she was still struggling for her mother's approval.

"Hi, Mom. Let's have a cup of coffee," Rita hugged Frances.

"What's the matter, nothing more important to do today than visit me?" Frances said, hugging her stiffly.

"I know you're really happy to see me, so why ask a question like that?" Rita reached for her cigarettes.

"Of course I'm happy to see you. You just walked in the door and already you're accusing me of saying something wrong," Frances changed the subject, "How's Steven doing?"

"Steven's fine, They asked me to be with them when the baby's born."

"Are you going to help out like a good grandmother, or are you going to stay here and dedicate yourself to your adoring public?" Frances fumbled with the coffee pot at the stove.

Rita sat at the formica kitchen table and begged, "Please, Mom, don't do this, okay?"

"Okay! I just want to be sure you know how I feel about the responsibility that comes with being a grandmother," Frances reached for one of Rita's cigarettes, lit it, and inhaled, saying, "You just can't keep living in sin with a man ten years younger than yourself, and expect your grandchildren to respect you, that's all."

"For God's sake, stop it!" Rita flushed, "I'm finally happy, living with someone I love and I am not going to let you belittle me or run my life. I'm a grown-up." Rita inhaled her cigarette, feeling like a twelve-year-old.

"How does Phil feel about your living in sin?"

"It's Peter, Mother, PETER!" Rita felt the veins in her neck swelling. She put her cigarette out in the ashtray.

"What kind of man is he, anyway?"

"PETER is a wonderful, sensitive man who adores me!" Rita was escalating despite her promise to herself to stay cool.

Frances did not listen or hear her. She absentmindedly put out her cigarette in her saucer.

Rita watched in disgust.

"What did you say Phil did for a living? I always forget," Frances asked out of nowhere.

"Oh, for God's sake, Mom, stop this. PETER is a sculptor. He's a talented artist."

"So maybe he needs a rich lady lawyer to support him? Isn't that possible? Just because you still look like a young woman and you lie about your age, don't think time is on your side. You're still about to become a grandmother."

"What's that supposed to mean? If my son and his wife have a baby, I become an old woman? Does becoming a grandmother mean I'm going to wake up in the morning with solid grey hair, a fresh assortment of wrinkles, flab, and a touch of Alzheimer's?"

"Don't shout, Rita!" Frances ordered, "Being a grandmother is something to be happy about." She plopped down at the table.

"Does being a grandmother mean I'll be happier rocking in a

chair than romping in bed with Peter? Does having a grandbaby in my life condemn me to the role of a sexless, weak, withered, voiceless wimp of a woman whose only interested is how often she can babysit?" Rita was livid, her cheeks red, her eyes flashing.

"Is your grandchild going to use the name Flunk?" Frances asked the question without warning.

"Oh please, not that again. Steven's last name is Justice, just like mine."

"Whoever heard of making up a name from the encyclopedia? You divorce, you take back your maiden name! You don't make up a phony name like Justice." Frances jumped up from the table to get the sugar she knew neither of them used.

"Listen, I've only got an hour before I have to meet Peter, so either we stay civilized, or I'm leaving."

"I am civilized," Frances said, pouting, "I'm just hurt, that's all."

"About WHAT?"

"About you changing your name. That's what."

"Give me a break, that was twenty years ago!" Rita was sinking fast.

"So, I'm still hurt. Can I help it? You're the professional, you be the judge. Can people change the way they feel about something so disgusting as taking a phony name?"

"Damn it!" Rita yelled, "I'm absolutely sick of your twisting everything I do so that is looks contaminated."

Frances pointed her bony finger inches from Rita's face and said, "Go ahead, yell at me. I only tell you these things for your own good. Nobody else has the nerve."

Rita pushed her coffee cup away, "I'm through letting you criticize me. Do you understand? Either we say something nice or we shut up! Did you hear me?" Rita was loud.

"I hear you. You don't have to shout."

"I do have to shout! You can't even hear me when I scream! How do you expect me to talk to you in a whisper?"

"I'm still your mother. Don't you raise your voice to me in anger." Frances' glaring eyes widened like a bird about to peck it's prey.

"I'll raise my voice if I want to. There's nothing wrong with expressing anger. It's how I feel. I'm fucking furious!"

"Maybe if you didn't use words like a drunken sailor, I'd be proud of you."

"You'll never be proud of me because I'm not who you wanted me to be. I'm not living my life for you the way you would have liked it." Rita wanted to stop, but she couldn't.

"Don't tell me I'm not proud of you. I brag about you to everybody. I say how hard you've worked for your independence, how you've struggled to become a lady lawyer. No, it's not what I wanted for you. So what should I do, pretend to approve of your loose lifestyle?"

"My loose lifestyle!" Rita was aware of the sweat beading up around her mouth, of her heart pounding, "What does that mean? I'm as selective and moral as anyone. I've never even had a one-night stand. How dare you?"

"Your father and I both worried plenty about your overly sexual ways since you were a baby," Frances pointed her finger again. "We had to stop you from rolling around with your hands under you when you were just three years old."

"I used to roll on my hands when I was three and you were worried I was a sex pervert?!"

"That's not all," Frances said in a raspy whisper, as if safeguarding a secret, "You were always more interested in boys than anything else. When you were a teenager, we were afraid you would get pregnant."

Rita felt a knot tightening in her belly. She stared at her untouched coffee, wondering how her father had survived. Then she remembered - he hadn't.

"That's enough, Stop it! No more," Rita exploded," I'm leaving."

"Don't you dare leave here mad, Rita. You know how dangerous it is to leave on bad terms. One of us might be dead before we have a chance to make up."

Rita said through clenched teeth, "I've let you rave on with your stupid insinuations long enough."

Frances looked as if she'd been run over by a truck. "What did I say now?" She really didn't know. "Why is it I always wind up the bad one? I've sacrificed my whole life for my family and I always come out the **villain**. I'm the one who made real sacrifices!"

Rita screamed, "Who asked you to sacrifice yourself? Sacrificing yourself is just a way to control people. It's a trick to torture someone. Is it my fault you're the way your are?"

"How do I know? How do I know how I'd be if I hadn't had you?" Frances banged her spoon on the table so hard it fell to the floor.

"Are you complaining about having me?" Rita picked up the spoon from the floor and put it back on the table.

Frances was startled. "Am I complaining?" she whined.

"You're always complaining. You're either complaining, demanding, or scared."

"I'm an old woman. Can't you understand that?" Frances voice cracked.

"It isn't age that makes you old. It's attitude. You're an old woman because you're either complaining, demanding, or scared."

"So what should I do? Dance and sing through the house? I can't hear. I can't see. My husband's dead and my only daughter lives in sin and treats me like shit. I'm asking you, how should I act, grateful?"

"You've never been grateful in your life."

"You have no right to talk to me like that, Rita. I've been a good mother to you."

"Do you want me to tell you what I'm so angry about? Are you even curious, or would you rather we stay stupidly superficial until one of us drops dead and the survivor desperately attempts to figure out what went wrong?"

"Go ahead. Tell me all the things I've done wrong. Go on. I can take it. I've been hit by bigger bombs."

Rita pulled her chair close and looked into Frances' face. "I'm just an image to you. You expected me to do what you wanted to do, and couldn't. So whenever I do something you wouldn't do, you hate me for it."

"I've never hated you Rita, not for one minute, ever."

"I'm not sure it's possible to love anyone you're not sometimes free to hate."

"So this is the result of your going to some therapist for help. You now believe I've gone wrong because I've been unable to hate you properly. I failed motherhood because I don't know how to hate you?"

"I want to love you, Mom, but to be free to love you, I have to be me. And me is different from you. Do you understand that?"

"I understand we don't agree on some things."

"We don't agree on anything except that cigarette butts belong in ashtrays. You've taught me your rules, and I reject them!" Rita hoped Frances heard her.

"You reject me because I'm your mother?"

"Because I don't want to be like you! Look at yourself! It makes me sad to see so much die in a person while she's still alive."

"You think your way is better? You think you have the answers?"

"Why is it that everywhere else in the world I'm respected, admired, and loved, but with you I always feel guilty, ugly, and sinful. Why is it you never make me feel loved?"

"Of couse I love you, Rita. I just don't want you to embarrass me, that's all."

"Why do you think I'd embarrass you?"

"Because I know you, that's why," Frances said proudly.

"Oh no you don't!" Rita screamed, "You haven't the slightest idea who I am!" She was officially back to her six-year-old status.

"That's enough!" Frances screamed. "Shut up!"

"YOU SHUT UP!"

"I said that's enough! Go home now. Leave me be. You've done enough damage here for one day. What are you trying to do, give me a heart attack?" Frances began to cry.

Rita picked up her purse, walked to the front door, and opened it to leave.

Frances yelled to her, "So what do you want from me?"

Rita turned and saw her mother, standing stiff as a soldier. She took a deep breath to compose herself and said evenly, "Just a little love, Mom, just a little love."

"What?" Frances hollered, "I didn't hear you!"

RITA IN A GROUP

Rita came to a playshop after her friend, Peter, suggested she needed to learn to either tolerate France or disown her!

In the opening circle, Rita made excessive remarks and sounded like a typically defensive nervous woman who believed her only problem was her mother. She used her role as lady lawyer to persuade, influence, and seduce people into agreeing with her.

She blabbed her way through the first night, talking incessantly, stopping only long enough to smoke. She felt misplaced, misunderstood, and only identified with other smokers. Besides, everyone was told that in the morning when they awoke, they were to stay in SILENCE *(p. 47)* throughout the morning exercise session, and remain silent until breakfast, a situation Rita found intolerable.

Everything changed dramatically the next morning. After the group "circled up" for the first sessions after breakfast, they began with NEWS AND GOODS *(p. 46)*, a psychological trick enabling the mind to focus on something positive, especially useful in today's world, which is so filled with negativity. People sat in the circle and passed the talking stick, simply stating something that was New and Good for them that morning.

When it was Rita's turn she said glibly, "What's New and Good for me is that normally I have to wait until after my first cup of coffee to smoke, but this morning, since I knew I had to stock up enough nicotine to get me through the exercises, I managed to smoke three cigarettes before my coffee."

A few of her smoking buddies laughed.

Lucy, recognizing a plea for help, asked, "Do you enjoy smoking that much?"

"Oh, yes," came the reply, "I wake up every morning and thank God I'm a smoker."

Nobody laughed.

"I have an idea," Lucy offered, reaching behind her. "How about taking a real challenge?" And she handed Rita a big painted button.

Rita exclaimed, "On, no! I've tried to stop smoking a hundred times but I..."

Then, she read the button which read, "I'M IN SILENCE, THANKS."

"Thank goodness," Rita said with a sigh, "I thought you wanted me to stop smoking."

Lucy laughed. "Have you ever spent any time without talking, Rita?"

"What's the point of being silent, when you can talk?" Rita laughed nervously, "I talk to myself when I'm alone, and if that's not possible, I sing."

"Rita, take a deep breath," Lucy said gently, "Your challenge, should you accept it, is to remain in this playshop until the last morning, without saying another word. And know this," Lucy went on, "it's not possible to fail or even make a mistake in this playshop." Lucy was clear, "So if at any time you find Silence too difficult, you can turn in your button, and relax back to your normal role."

Rita said, "I can imagine that learning how to shut up once in a while may be a big assett to someone who earns her living wagging her tongue." Then the realization sank in, "Wait a minute," she said, "am I going to be the only one in Silence?"

Lucy smiled in confirmation, "You may find Silence is most effective when everyone else around you is talking."

And Rita accepted the challenge.

Silence was difficult at first, even maddening, for Rita. But people were so supportive, encouraging, and compassionate, that it wasn't long before she felt special, important, and accepted. She didn't have to prove herself with her usual patter. She began to love Silence even more than the challenge. Rita was discovering herself. The less defended she was, the more curious she became.

During one session, a young man named Max, who was around her son's age, was working on his relationship with his mother. He needed someone who reminded him of his own mother to "play" the role. He picked Rita.

She was asked to stand there and remain silent, so Max could direct his resentments toward his "mother."

As Max stood staring at Rita, she thought, "He could be Steven, he even looks like him."

Then Max screamed, "Where have you been all my life? Where were you when I broke my arm and when I won my soccer match? Why couldn't you love me?"

Rita heard Max's words and finally faced her own denied doubts about her son, Steven. Was his drug use her fault? His inability to finish school, or his lack of interest in anything besides his computer her fault? Had he gotten married so young because of problems that were her fault? Were his problems a function of growing up, or her fault?

Suddenly, Rita wanted to know that she'd been a good mother. She needed reassurance that she was loved.

Max, his hands clenched in fists, screamed, "You've been a bitch all your life."

Lucy said, "Mothers don't have to win personality contests. They're ordinary people, and just as scared as their kids."

Rita thought, "My mother's personality could convert Gandhi to violence, but she's no more scared than I am."

Max, still facing Rita, screamed again, "I want my freedom! Let me go!"

Lucy said firmly, "No one can give you your freedom, you have to take it."

Max yelled, "But why won't you let me go?"

Lucy said, "She's too afraid to let you go. She's too afraid of life without you. You have to leave her. Then you'll be free to love and protect her."

Rita thought, "Steven's free of me, that's why I know he loves me. And I'm free. I've got nobody to blame for anything anymore. Frances will never change, but I can change the way I react to her."

Max screamed again, "I love you, damn it...I love you." And he screamed again and again, until at last, worn out and exhausted, the rage gone from his belly, he reached out to Rita and they hugged and held each other as they wept away the pain of the past. Rita and surrogate son relaxed into mutual acceptance and love.

As the session ended, Rita wished she could call Steven, just to hear him say, "I love you," but she remembered...she was in Silence.

The next night, everyone played a role in costume. They played the person who had given them the most trouble in life. People were dressed as children, old folks, and fantasy figures. Some played parents, others lovers, spouses, and siblings. The atmosphere was light-hearted and fun.

Rita played her mother. She dressed herself in someone's long black skirt, covered her hair with powder so it was completely white, and painted a black mole at the side of her nose, even though Frances had had hers removed. She didn't dance, she didn't smile, she didn't talk. She sat with her arms folded, being critical. By acting tough like Frances, Rita realized what it was like to play a role that excludes flexibility, tolerance, and curiosity, and she saw the tragedy of her mother's life.

Later in the evening, women and men divided into separate circles. With her eyes closed, Rita listened to the instructions, "Look at this person you've been role playing all evening, this person who is so important in your life, and see the goddess in her."

Rita laughed. She tried imagining her mother as a goddess. She couldn't.

The she heard, "A goddess is an ordinary woman when she's unafraid" *(Moore, 1988)*.

Rita could never remember a time when Frances was unafraid. Oh, once or twice perhaps, when she'd had a little too much sherry, but then she would over-compensate by being twice as scared the next day, for fear she may have embarrassed herself.

Then she heard, "A goddess is an ordinary woman who has found her soul."

Rita knew that Frances thought soul was music to which black people danced.

Then she heard, "A goddess is an ordinary woman who often tries to play roles culture insists she play."

Rita saw herself then, struggling with the roles of daughter, mother, lover, lawyer, soon-to-be-grandmother.

Then she saw Frances, who played the role her parents created for her, despite the tragedy of the drama; Frances, the good little girl who grew up believing the lies so she never found the truth.

"A goddess in an ordinary woman who, despite what anybody thinks, is doing the best she can."

Rita saw Frances again, an ordinary woman doing the best she could, struggling to be loved.

Then she saw herself, an ordinary woman who resisted the roles society had inflicted on her, struggling not to loose her identity, her essence, in the name of a role. She saw herself, defensive lawyer, rebellious child, angry mother. No wonder she resisted the grandmother role; it meant losing the goddess she'd been searching for.

"A goddess is flexible and bends like the willow; a goddess is tolerant, and feels compassion; a goddess obeys cosmic law and follows her intuition. She's receptive, curious. A goddess is a woman who is free to love."

Rita saw Frances among the last of a dying breed, a woman so busy playing roles, she never saw the goddess inside.

Rita breathed and let out her sadness. No wonder she'd stayed angry at Frances. IT WAS LESS PAINFUL TO BE ANGRY THAN SAD.

"A goddess is an ordinary woman when somebody loves her."

Rita heard the words through her tears. She saw herself with Frances. She saw both of them screaming, frustrated, afraid they'd failed, pretending not to give a damn, and not feeling loved at all.

She cried as several people held and comforted her. When she'd cried enough, Rita smiled, wishing she could call Frances and tell her that she was a goddess because she was loved. Then Rita remembered that she was in Silence.

The next morning, Rita awoke feeling peaceful and relaxed and she wasn't dying for a cigarette. She craved the nicotine, but her intention not to smoke was strong and so was her will power. As she took a cigarette out of the package, a sweet little smile spread like ivy across her face, and she dropped the cigarettes into the garbage pail on the way to exercise.

It was the last morning of the playshop and Rita's turn to do News and Goods. She took off her button, slowly, proudly, and before she could say a word, everyone clapped and cheered. People got up and hugged her. She had made it! She'd spent three full days and nights in a group of people without saying a word!

Finally, she took the talking stick and said, "What's New and Good for me is that I found my Self in Silence."

Some people were moved to tears.

"I see my life as a tape recorder, mostly on fast forward with occasional pauses. Silence put me on stop long enough to rewind, so now I can spend more time on play."

People applauded.

She went on, "And it's great and new to be a non-smoker."

Everyone cheered.

"And," she said, her eyes brimming with tears, "it's New and Good to know that my son will one day say of me, 'She was a goddess who did the best she could and I love her.'"

RITA AS A LEADER

After the playshop, three people who had determined to stop smoking formed a SUPPORT GROUP (*see p. 48*) They met bi-weekly for a few months in Rita's home, until all three managed to quit smoking.

They learned more than how to stop smoking. They began rotating group leadership with each meeting and turned the group into an exciting, educational, and inspiring gathering.

People began hearing about the Support Group, and within eight months, there were twenty-eight people who had stopped smoking and who still came to occasional meetings for fun, to see their friends, or to inspire the beginners who needed support. By this time, the group was meeting monthly in different members' homes.

Rita was now an ardent non-smoker. Her mother, Frances, had lung cancer, her father had already died of cancer, and a strong-willed, impassioned Rita was fast becoming politically active against the tobacco industry's deceitful advertising practices.

Rita arrived late and exhausted to one gathering of the Support Group. If it hadn't been her turn to be the leader, and if it hadn't been held at her own house, she definitely wouldn't have gone. She'd spent the day at the hospital, where Frances lay close to death. They'd become very close since the diagnosis, and Rita was feeling the pain of her mother's demise.

Rita began the meeting by taking the Talking Stick and saying, "It's New and Good to be able to stop acting like Superwoman and to admit that right now I feel very sad. My mother is dying." Fighting her tears, Rita continued, "She is dying from a preventable disease, lung cancer, probably caused by smoking cigarettes."

The woman sitting next to Rita turned toward her and Rita let herself be held as she cried. Finally, she said, blowing her nose, "I need your support for a new law to force the cigarette companies to caution consumers about the addictive properties of nicotine."

She breathed again, "And I want to present documented case histories of people who've tried to stop, and couldn't. Please write a short description of your own experience with smoking and mail it to me as soon as possible."

Applause and exclamations filled the room as Rita passed the stick to a young pregnant woman.

"My name is Barbara, and it's New and Good for me to sit in a group of non-smokers and feel great knowing my baby won't be born addicted, as I was, because my mother smoked when she carried me."

There were cheers and affirmations as she passed the stick to a grey-haired man in his sixties, who suffered from emphysema.

The man took the stick slowly, saying, "New and Good is knowing there is a group of people curious enough to wonder why nicotine, one of the most lethal, deadly, and addicitive drugs in the world, is legal!"

Applause exploded, especially from the "research committee." While studying nicotine, they had discovered that no research was published about a drug often more difficult to withdraw from than heroin.

After the stick had gone halfway around, a fiesty woman with an unsmiling face, who was there for the first time, took the stick and said, "I'm Kay, and despite the peer pressure, I believe people have the right to smoke if they choose."

Her words hit Rita like the snowflake that breaks the bough.

Rita said, "Of course people have the right to smoke, AND they have the right to know that they may not be able to stop smoking when they want to!"

"People can stop smoking when they want to," Kay responded flatly.

Rita replied, "The habit of smoking is one problem, the addiciton to nicotine is another!" Then, as group leader, she stopped herself from talking too much, and asked calmly, "Kay, do you want to say anything else, or are you ready to pass the stick?"

Kay responded with, "I need to stop smoking, but I take responsibility for my own habits. I want to leave the laws up to lawyers; they're none of my business. I intend to stop smoking!"

Rita bit her lip until the stick made its way back to her. Then, pulling together what little remaining energy she had, she looked around slowly, making eye contact with everyone in the circle, and said, "Until recently, I used my role as lawyer to get what I thought I needed. I focused my blind rage on my mother to keep from seeing that in reality, if I told the truth, the whole truth, and nothing but the truth, I'd be arrested. I thought the role of lawyer meant driving big cars in the fast lane and learning to lie with conviction. My mother was the only one telling me the truth about myself. Who else but a mother dares to tell us the truth? So naturally I couldn't stand her."

A hush had fallen over the circle.

"Then," Rita said softly, "in the safety of a Support Group, I was able to see myself for who I really was, and I got my first little look at the big picture. It wasn't willpower that helped me stop smoking, it was compassion."

Then Rita stopped and said, "Will each of you please face someone sitting next to you."

Everyone faced a partner.

"Please take a breath. Don't worry, it's safe. Nobody's smoking here."

A little ripple of laughter circled the air.

"Now, will you please look at each other? Look into each other's eyes. We need each other. We are all ordinary people trying to survive in a world filled with destructive toxic products, from tobacco to nuclear weapons. If it's destructive and causes death, it's immoral. It's immoral to seduce young people into an addiction that can kill them. It's immoral to sit by and deny that it's happening. We can change man-made laws. The cosmic law, the basic law of morality, is the law we have to trust. Please, reach out and give your partner a hug, because we need each other."

The group ended happily, but Rita couldn't sleep.

The next morning, Frances died with a smile on her face, her hand in Rita's.

RITA'S ACTIVITIES
News And Goods

One amazingly powerful way to begin a group is to ask people to state clearly and succinctly, something that is New and Good for them at that moment.

In a Support Group, for example, besides insuring a positive attitude, doing News and Goods provides everyone an equal opportunity to share.

In a classroom, doing News and Goods with children gives them a better understanding of each other; in a group of colleagues, sharing something personally New and Good provides a warmth not usually present in professional settings.

Personally, with a friend on the phone, or a partner you live with, getting up in the morning and telling each other something that's New and Good, guarantees at least a few minutes of gratitude, communion, or good humor.

With an aging parent who tends to be critical or demanding, sharing something New and Good limits the amount of negativity that normally drives us crazy. Add a little humor, and life takes on new meaning.

The human mind is difficult to control. We have two choices: we either learn to control it, or the mind controls US. Focusing on what's New and Good teaches us how to think positively. It works when you're alone, with a parent or partner, with friends, or in a group.

Silence

Silence is a method for listening to the greatest teacher of all, that pure white light of truth that often screams to be heard. But most of us are so busy trying to survive our crazy culture, we either don't have time to listen, or we're afraid (unconsciously, of course) that if we stop and hear that small still voice inside, we won't be able to continue our basically boring, destructive, and senseless lifestyles.

Extremely talkative group members often find spending a portion of their group time in Silence a valuable experience. They "hear" their defensiveness when they're silent, and learn ways of belonging that are less toxic to themselves and those around them.

As an activity for the whole group, Silence for a specified period in the morning or before a group session disrupts unconscious habitual behavior patterns and can allow participants to center themselves and be aware of their energy in a way that is not usually possible.

As a group activity during a break, partners can take a walk together in Silence, only interacting non-verbally with gestures and grunts to express what they need, want, and intend in that moment. This provides a clarity and focus not normally possible with everyday chatter.

So little of what we believe is a result of original thinking. A way to discover the truth of how little you actually KNOW, is to spend some time in Silence. Get a group of friends together for one day, and only speak to each other when you can share something you KNOW, not what you think. It's amazing and enlightening to discover how little we know.

Since people are more afraid of change than anything else, silence is often seen as something to avoid. But in silence, we can hear the truth about ourselves, each other, and the world we live in, and we can "change" what no longer serves our highest intentions *(Yogananda, 1981)*. In silence, we hear the truth, and God is truth.

Support Groups

Gatherings of people who consciously support each other's needs, wants, and intentions are known as Support Groups. Groups "support" each other by sharing and rewarding successes, and range from world-wide organization like Alcoholics Anonymous to informal gatherings of friends in someone's home. They can offer fun, excitement, inspiration, personal growth, and even life-saving support. For example, the vast majority of AIDS patients in some cultures rely totally on support from volunteers, because they are not supported by their government. Without financial assistance and humane support, people with AIDS would not be able to die with dignity. Support Groups can motivate people to go on. It's hard to keep trying when you feel nobody cares.

Consider the importance of Support Groups for:

- ▶ those injured by chemical or radiation poisoning, with little information about how to get treatment *(Gofman, 1981)*.
- ▶ women with unwanted pregnancies, confronting abortion.
- ▶ car-pooling, for those wanting to contribute to the health of the environment, but who need a ride to work.
- ▶ people who need support to endure the loss of a loved one.

- newly divorced people, singles, parents without partners.
- food co-oping so families can eat better, for less.
- newly unemployed people - the nouveau poor.
- people withdrawing from drugs and alcohol.
- people facing cancer.

Often when we seek "medical" help for the normal problems of sadness, depressions, and anger, we find ourselves in the role of patient and rely on someone else to fix us. But people are primarily, fundamentally healthy and beautiful, and our responses are legitimate. For example, most depression is reactive, anger turned inward. No one can be unaffected by the plight of the planet today, and denial is only a sympton of despair. The next time you think you're alone, remember - we need each other.

CHAPTER 4

RICHARD HEART'S LOVE

Richard was afraid to open his heart. His parents were unaffectionate, afraid of touching, and his love for his sister had been sexual. He was confused about love and friendship. His pain for the planet was intense, and his depression a natural reaction to the options that face all young people today. When he faced his despair, he opened his heart and fell in love. Richard understood the need for therapeutic therapists, began studying psychology, and intended to do therapy in groups.

RICHARD AT A CROSSROADS

Nobody would believe that likeable, intelligent, good-looking Richard Heart would decide to spend the rest of his life in bed. While a student at the university, he'd joked about how nice it would be to never leave the house, but after his graduation, he simply was not motivated to get out of bed.

The bitter cold winds howling outside his one-bedroom flat drove Richard deeper under the down comforter, until only his noble nose peeked out. He was shivering, his chest ached, he was short of breath, and he felt lonely. The cat had abandoned the messy apartment when he had run out of cat food. Richard wished for a girlfriend, but any friend would do. Just as he was wondering why, at twenty-three, he felt like an old man with nothing to hold on to except his penis, his sister Regina called.

"Are you sick?" Regina asked in her I'm-two-years-older-than-you tone.

"I'm sick of everything, Regina, but don't worry, no one will ever know. They'll never notice because I'm not going to leave my apartment." Richard caught her off guard. He was usually the better adjusted of the two.

"We need to talk, Richard. I want to know what's going on. Besides, I haven't seen you in months."

"If you come over here you'll catch terminal nausea. This place is such a wreck the cat left. By the way, bring some cat food."

An hour later Regina walked in Richard's messy flat carrying cat food and a pizza. Her straight, long blond hair framed her porcelain, picture-perfect face. Her bright blue eyes always grabbed Richard's attention and went straight to his heart.

"I would have come over sooner," Regina said smiling, looking at his long, dark, disheveled hair trailing off the edge of his pillow, "but when you've seen one depressed person, you've seen them all."

Richard burrowed deeper beneath the covers.

"Richard!" Regina said authoritatively, "Get out of bed!" And she went to the kitchen and put the pizza on the table.

"Why?" he yelled to her.

"Because I'm your older sister and I know you've been in that damn bed smoking marijuana all day."

"I haven't used any marijuana! I'm too depressed to get high. Besides, I don't smoke it. I eat it in sugar-free granola."

"Why do you use it at all?" Regina asked irritably.

"Because I cannot survive the stresses of a world of terrorists, chemical poisoning, economic insecurity, and the threat of nuclear incineration without relief from that awareness."

"I still think drugs are bad news."

"That's because you're brainwashed. You lump all mind-altering substances into one category, label it 'drugs' and then blindly convert innocent people to criminals. It's a smart political move because people are easy to control when they feel guilty" (*Hoffman, 1987, Trebach, 1987*).

"Marijuana is not the answer to the problems of the world," Regina was annoyed.

"At least it's not lethal like alcohol and nicotine."

"That's not funny!" Regina scowled, "It's illegal, Richard!"

"That depends on where you live!" Richard yelled, losing patience.

Regina was confused. Richard was normally the less-opinionated of the two.

Richard sat up, propped his pillow behind his head, and said, "I am NOT willing to go unquestioningly into a world of AIDS; poisoned air, food and water; polluted morals; AND participate in the rat race - get up, go to work, come home tired, get up, go to work, come home tired, get up, go to work..."

"I think you're just lonely."

"And you've come to cheer me up? Isn't that what you used to do when we were kids, Regina, come over and cheer me up?"

"Wait a minute," Regina said, agitated, "Why go back to when we were kids? What's that got to do with now?"

"Everything!" Richard stood up, escalating, "Why not go back to when we were kids? That's when it all started, isn't it?"

"Is it?" Regina asked, defensively.

Richard sat down and picked at a piece of lint on his robe. He could still see Regina at ten or twelve, when it first began, standing there in her little flannel nightshirt that allowed the faintest hint of her baby body to show. He had been alternately curious and timid, intrigued by her cute, cunning ways, and she had invited him into her bed to share the shades of darkness. It was an innocent seduction. His fascination grew and his love grew, and didn't stop.

Regina said, "You remember too much. It's time to forget."

"How can I forget?" Richard stood up, "I loved you in a sick, crazy, desperate way. You were older! You should have known better! You should have stopped it before it went too far."

"You can't keep blaming me for what happened with us," Regina pleaded, "We were who we were to each other, and we were only children - babies! Stop blaming me and start taking some responsibility for yourself. I'm not to blame, WE ARE. And besides, I know some things now that I didn't know before I got some help about this stuff."

"What do you mean?" Richard asked, sitting back down on the bed and watching her closely.

"I mean I've learned that what we experienced...did... together, was not so unusual, or sick. It's quite common. We need to forgive ourselves and one another, and love each other again as brother and sister."

"Sisterly love, to me, is quite different than for most men," Richard was cautious, "so be careful when you suggest that I love you like a sister."

"I don't want to be afraid to touch you, Richard. I love you. I want to bury the past, please!" Regina said, sitting directly in front of him.

"That sounds so simple. I wish it were that easy for me. I've suffered a lot." He stood up dramatically.

"Stop bobbing up and down like a yo-yo!" Regina snapped impatiently. She got to her feet. "I've had a hard time and done a lot of soul searching, too, but I really have let it go."

"Maybe it's easier for you because I was the one who stood there choking on my tears, watching you walk out the door with your boyfriend."

Regina softened, "I'm sorry for everything that's happened between us. We've made mistakes. That was years ago. Now let's forgive and forget, okay? I love you. You're my brother." Regina reached out to hug him.

Insecure, Richard sidestepped her, saying, "I'm not sure I know what love is. At our house I though love meant new things, a new sweater, shoes, a sports car."

"I know what you mean. I would have been happier if Mom or Dad would have said, 'I love you,' just once."

Richard let himself look at Regina, "I've heard you have to love yourself before you can love anyone else, but maybe you have to feel somebody loves you before you can love yourself." He sat back down on the bed resting his chin on his hand.

"What are you thinking about?"

"I'm thinking about what I'm going to do with the rest of my life," he said soberly.

"How long is that going to take? The pizza's getting cold."

RICHARD IN A GROUP

Richard arrived early the day the playshop began. Walking around the grounds, he thought, "I wonder why I'm so insecure about women?" He thought about Regina and blamed her.

"Why is it I can't understand people any better than they seem to understand me?" He thought about his alcoholic father and blamed him for everything from the weather to world hunger.

"I'm really not afraid of not being able to love or be loved." He wondered about his unaffectionate mother and why she couldn't say, "I love you."

He thought about his options for a career in a corrupt culture, and visualized himself crucified while crusading for justice in the hospital where his father operated.

Richard Heart's Love

He wondered, "What if I can't overcome my apathy?" and thought, "I'm not apathetic, I'm hopeless and bored. I don't want to swim in the mainstream because it's polluted."

He pondered the chaos in the world and worried, "Can the planet survive?" And then he wondered if he would survive the playshop.

At 7 o'clock that evening, in the opening circle, Richard said, "I'm here because my sister promised to clean my apartment if I came to this playshop..."

Everybody laughed.

He continued, "...and to figure out what I'm going to do with the rest of my life."

By 9 o'clock, he was looking at his partner. Richard was opposite an ordinary goddess, with extraordinary red hair, freckles, and stars in her big blue eyes.

Just as he was thinking, "Somehow she reminds me of Regina," the woman said, "I'm Roseann."

"I'm Richard," he smiled nervously into her adorable face.

They were sitting cross-legged on comfortable cushions on a wonderful wooden floor, their hands resting on each other's knees. Neither of them knew what was coming or what they were about to do. Lucy's instructions were simply to breathe deeply and look into each other's eyes.

Richard and Roseann heard, "This person sitting opposite of you is not your sister, brother, old friend, or parent. This is a human being, like you, living on an endangered planet, trying to survive."

Richard felt a wave of excitement. He wasn't the only one worried about the Earth.

"Please take a breath and relax. You have nothing to worry about for the next five minutes..."

Richard and Roseann giggled nervously.

"It is a great privilege to look deep into someone's eyes, someone's soul. Let yourself take a deep breath and keep looking. Human beings are an endangered species. We are faced with annihilation, living on the brink of nuclear war, witnessing the destruction of our support systems, like our air, food, and water."

Richard wondered if his parents knew, or cared, about what was happening to the planet.

"The person you're sitting with is no exception. Please drop your prejudices and pre-conditioned responses."

Richard thought, "So what if she dyes her hair red, and her teeth are a little crooked?" and he smiled, feeling proud of himself.

"This is a member of your race, the human race."

Richard thought, "Odd, I've always thought of myself as a member of the white race, not the human race."

"If the human race is to survive, we must become flexible, tolerant, and curious."

Richard thought, "I'm not flexible, I'm stiff. I'm not tolerant, I'm prejudiced as hell. At least I'm curious."

"This person, like yourself, is lonely now and then, and gets tired and frightened and angry sometimes. Please keep looking into your partner's eyes.

Richard couldn't take his eyes from hers if he tried. He was glued to her.

"Let yourself see this human being with kindness and compassion, and without words, offer them solace."

Richard's heart pounded as he and Roseann reached out to embrace each other. They helped one another without judgements, criticisms, or thought. He had only just met this woman whose eyes reflected his own fear and anger, and yet they hugged each other so lovingly, with such compassion, they felt safe.

Throughout the day, Richard and Roseann flirted, played, fantasized, danced, and feigned indifference to each other. Clearly no one was surprised when they chose each other as partners that night to do stress-releasing body work *(Namikoshi, 1985)*.

The group room was warm. A cozy fire roared in the huge stone fireplace, soft music filled the air, and mattresses, cushions, and blankets were everywhere.

Richard whispered to Roseann, "This is the first time I've ever done anything like this. I hope you're not expecting much. I can hardly manage the stress in my own body."

Richard worked on Roseann first. Fully dressed in soft cotton clothes, she was relaxed and trusting. She lay on her back on a mattress, her magnificent red hair cascading around her head.

At one point, he held Roseann's head and slowly rotated it

from one side to the other, so slowly, so imperceptibly, that he could literally feel her "losing her head." It thrilled him for her to relax so deeply, and sigh with such intense pleasure.

When he massaged her face she relaxed even more, and each stroke of his fingers brought sighs and moans.

When he'd finished, Roseann looked up at Richard gratefully, "You'd make a wonderful therapist."

"Oh yeah? How come?" he asked, delighted, wondering if it was because he hadn't had a single sexual thought while he'd worked on her.

"I don't know. You just would."

Later, Roseann worked on Richard. He was lying on his belly. She knelt, straddling his torso, her knees on either side of his hips, and with her elbow began tracing a line from his shoulder to the middle of his back. She gradually increased pressure until Richard began moaning.

Her elbow was the fuel that rocketed him back in time. The deeper she went, the more frequent the flashes of incidents, both grand and grim. Images appeared of little Richard, a pint-sized alien in his lonely little world, images of himself wanting to be touched and held.

"Mommy! Mommy!" He saw himself at age six, begging for attention, his knees scraped and bloody. But no one came, except Regina, who had begun to take care of him.

Roseann dug her elbow deeper and he saw himself at age seven. A nightmare had awakened him, the scary images still clinging to his sleepy head. He needed comforting. Instead he heard, "Get back to bed this minute!" Again it was Regina who soothed him.

Roseann's elbow dug into the muscles of his buttocks. He was eight. Smack! Wham! His father's drunken hand. And for nothing, he was being hit for nothing! His father was too drunk to realize he was supposed to be punishing Regina. But Regina told the truth and rescued him.

Deeper, Roseann pushed deeper into the old traumas until she went so deep, Richard had to let go. "Ahhhhhh!" he screamed, as the memories of so many childhood experiences, buried in the very cells of his body, faded.

Roseann held him in her arms, as he wept. Later he looked at her gratefully and asked, "Why do you think I'd make a good therapist?"

She gave him a warm, friendly smile, "Maybe because you've suffered enough."

The next morning during News and Goods, Richard shared the truth. "What's New and Good for me," he said brightly, "is that I have fallen in love."

People clapped and looked at Roseann, who had turned as red as her hair.

For the next few days, Richard found it impossible to worry. So much was happening around him.

He had learned how to control his thoughts by focusing on specific needs, wants, and intentions.

During the evening session, a singer played her guitar and the group sang:

> "The planet is crying...crying and dying.
> The planet is trying to survive.
> Sister and brother, help one another.
> Father and mother, help the children stay alive."

As Richard sang, the floodgates of compassion opened. He could feel love all around him. It was tangible, an undeniable energy. The haunting melody opened him up. The powerful message let him feel his pain for the planet - for his family, his people, for himself.

Richard cried. Everyone did.

Lather that night, after much comforting, holding, and healing, Richard and Roseann, too exhausted and too excited to sleep, stayed up to process what had happened that day. They grabbed a bottle of apple juice, raided the refrigerator, and sprawled on the carpeted group room floor like kids at a slumber party.

Richard was lying on his side, propped up on one elbow, resting on a stack of pillows. Roseann snuggled next to him, her head cradled against his belly.

Roseann said, "It's difficult for some people to be loving without being sexual."

Richard was trying to pay attention to her words, but as she reached over to get the juice, her great long legs and cute ass distracted him.

"We're all afraid to touch each other because we're afraid of our sexuality," Roseann went on intensely, pouring the juice. "We don't know how to handle love or sex. We think the opposite of love is hate, but it's not; it's fear."

"What's the opposite of hate, then?" Richard asked seriously.

Roseann said, "The opposite of hate is tolerance. Until people learn tolerance, they'll keep on hating. Until that happens, people can't understand the difference between love as energy and love as emotion."

"Can't we love someone energetically and emotionally?" Richard asked, wondering if he should feel guilty for wanting Roseann sexually.

"Sure, there's nothing wrong with wanting something from someone you love. What are you thinking?" Roseann asked softly, playing with his long hair.

"I'm thinking what a phony I am pretending I don't want you," Richard said, disarming them both.

Roseann smiled, "I'm confused, too. My mind doesn't want to hear what my heart is saying."

Richard turned on his side to look at her, "What's your heart saying?"

"My heart's saying, 'I love you,' energetically, of course." She gently kissed his lips.

Richard's heart raced. "What's your mind saying?" He managed to ask.

"My mind's telling me that casual sex went out with AIDS. I don't know what you want with me, and I'm afraid of being hurt."

Richard thought a minute, and as they snuggled on the mattress in the middle of the empty room he said, "I need to be loved. I want to be your friend and love you. I intend to give our friendship a chance to grow into a permanent partnership."

Looking into Richard's eyes, Roseann said, "I need to be loved. I want to love you. I intend to become friends before being lovers."

Richard held her sweet red head close to his heart and said, "I think friendship and love may be the salvation of us all."

RICHARD AS A LEADER

After the playshop, Richard's intention was clear: he wanted to be a therapist. He enrolled in a graduate school far from home. One year and two playshops later, he wrote the following letter to his sister.

Dear Regina,

Thanks to you, I'm on my way to becoming a therapist. I'm learning and growing despite my often intolerant attitude. I'm basically happy. Life is intense and love makes it all worth while. I know you'll be happy to hear that Roseann and I are planning to marry after I graduate.

As you know, no degree in the world can make me therapeutic, but a degree is my passport into the land of human behavior, and it's important to make legal entries into new frontiers. I'm determined to learn the body of knowledge of psychology so I can formulate my own theories about what works and what doesn't. So far, one of the most imporant things I've learned is when NOT to work with someone. So, I won't ever try to be your therapist, I'm more intersted in being your friend. It's clear to me now that you have always been my friend.

When I began to lead groups with hospitalized alcoholics (there was a doctor who reminded me of Dad), I discovered the body tells the truth. I can't heal someone I can't touch. Leaving the body out of psychology is like having a wedding without a bride! That's when I realized how difficult it must have been for Dad to learn to shut his heart to his patients -to treat only a sympton, not a person. His training toughened him up, and destroyed his capacity for compassion.

I have been using a system which helps me understand myself, my patients, and my friends better, and I want to share it with you. It's called TRI-ENERGETICS *(p. 62)*. I think you may find the system useful, too.

Problems arise from being inflexible in the body, intolerant in the mind and emotions, or not curious in the spirit. Tri-Energetics lets me be creative, and use any therapy or technique that works.

In my groups, whenever I'm stuck not knowing quite what to ask, or how to answer, I ask, "What do you need? What do you want? What do you intend?" or I consider the qualities of flexibility, tolerance, and curiosity and ask, "How flexible are you? How tolerant are you? Are you curious?"

Well, last night I got to thinking about you and me, and decided to get clear on what I needed, wanted, and intended with US. Here goes: "I NEED my sister. I WANT to be your friend. I INTEND for us to be friends and love each other. I WANT you to visit Roseann and me. I'm FLEXIBLE! Come when you can. I'm TOLERANT! If you can't come for Christmas, I understand. Are you healthy, happy, and in love? I'm CURIOUS!" Sharing this system with you is my way to reach out and to let you know who I am, now - your happy, though sometimes sad, brother.

Remember how we loved singing in the rain when we were kids?
I recently wrote:

> *I'm singing in the rain,*
> *A little acid rain.*
> *Add some radiation,*
> *And there goes my brain.*
> *It's really insane,*
> *Why cause all this pain?*
> *I'm singin' and cryin'*
> *In the rain.*

I know what happened to us, but whatever happened to the rain?
In my groups, we acknowledge the truth. I'm helping people see that it's normal to be depressed. Depression cannot be treated as if the world around us isn't depressing. People ARE planning to blow up the world! Civilization is crumbling! We have maybe fifteen years left! If these things don't make us sad, maybe we're still sleeping.
I'm waking up. It's just my luck to be waking up at the worst time in the history of the world. I used to think only a fool thought he could change the world; now I know only a fool thinks he can't.
I guess I'm just searching for a way to say that I think the wounds of our relationship have been healed. I love you.

Richard

Make the Circle Bigger

ACTIVITIES
Tri-Energetics

Tri-Energetics is a science of human energy; a simple, not always easy way of discovering who we are, where we're going, and why. It helps simplify the way we think, so we can become more aware of our intentions. It can be used for self-help, or by professionals as a clinical intervention. Anyone can use it.

Tri-Energetics is based on the unity of the soma-psyche-spirit, and embraces all therapies that work. It contains no dogma; there are no beliefs required. It is an open-ended system that promotes original thought.

The system consists of:
> three aspects - *soma, psyche, spirit*
> three functions - *need, want, intend*
> three attitudes - *flexible, tolerant, curious*

SOMA	Physical body.
PSYCHE	Mind and emotions.
SPIRIT	Soul.
NEED	Necessary for life, safety, and well-being.
WANT	Desire or wish. Frustration brings anger or longing.
INTEND	Conscious choice.
FLEXIBLE	Able to bend without breaking. Essential for the body.
TOLERANT	Accepting, inprejudiced, giving, and compassionate.
CURIOUS	Interested in knowing. Opposite of defensive. Required for living spiritually. No curiosity - no spirit.

> *Soma needs flexibility.*
> *Psyche wants tolerance.*
> *Spirit intends curiousity.*

Those who are flexible bend, the tolerant give, the curious know - they get the message. If you're flexible, you can bend AND you can stand straight. If you can't bend, you break. Give with love; the more you give, the more you have. If you can't give, you can't live. Know that only the curious get the message. And if you aren't curious, you're dead. Everything's dogma.

First, ask yourself, "What do I need?" Then, "What do I want?" Our needs and wants are often incompatible, i.e., "I need some rest. I want to go to a party." Then ask yourself, "What's my intention?" If you know what you need, and consciously follow your intentions, chances are you'll get what you want!

Write down what your body needs, what your heart wants, and what your soul is intending. Invite some friends over and do the the same activity in a group. Discussing each other's Tri-Energetics can be fun, engaging, and a way to know each other better.

Sing, *"I need la la la la,*
I want la la la la,
I intend la la la la la la..."
and fill in the blanks with a song. For example:
"I need to be loved,
I want to make a new friend,
I intend to find a friend I can love, who loves me."

Using the ego states from Transactional Analysis *(Berne 1978)*, complete the thought,
"The parent in me needs...wants...intends;
The adult in me needs...wants...intends;
The child in me needs...wants...intends."

If you're having difficulty in a relationship with someone, ask yourself, what does this person need, what does she want, and what's her intention? See how much easier it is to understand what's happening?

In a difficult situation, ask yourself how flexible you are, how tolerant, how curious. If you want to understand yourself better, see how flexible, tolerant, and curious you are. If you want to understand something or someone else better, check their levels of flexibility, tolerance, and curiosity.

Tri-Energetics can be used with little or no knowledge of the chakras or levels of consciousness, but using the chakras can provide the basis for a deep understanding of the complex physical, mental/emotional, and spiritual aspects of people.

Chakras are energy centers, vibrating at different frequencies, that can be seen as levels of consciousness. They are associated with the endocrine glands, which produce the hormones we need to become conscious.

The Lower Triad *(Chakras 1,2,3)* is primarily concerned with what the soma needs: survival, sex, and power. When the fourth chakra is active, the body becomes flexible. Love as an energy transforms the lower chakras by re-defining the consciousness. Survival becomes an issue of global preservation rather than self-indulgence, sexuality becomes transcendent and sacred, will-power becomes good will.

The Middle Triad *(Chakras 3,4,5)* is involved with what the psyche wants: power, love, and communication. Love brings tolerance to the mind and emotions.

The Upper Triad *(Chakras 5,6,7)* deals with communication, intuition, and enlightenment. When love flows through the upper triad, spirit becomes curious about the intentions of the soul. Communicaiton becomes communion, intuition becomes wisdom, and cosmic connection brings heaven to earth.

List the chakras, one through seven, and see what you need, want, and intend in each level of consciousness. In a group, discuss world leaders or other famous, influential people, and determine their level of consciousness based on their flexibility-tolerance-curiousity, or on what they need-want-intend. Do the same for your mother-in-law, your boss, your pet, your role model. Make it a game: Name That Chakra.

CHAPTER 5

SOPHIA SINGER'S COMMUNICATION

Sophia needed to listen to her inner voice, which was screaming to be heard. Her talents, like her intelligence and spirit, had been belittled and ignored by her over-controlling, abusive husband, and she was withering like a plant without water.

Within the safety of a group, she realized she needed acknowledgement, understanding, and communion. When she experienced them, she discovered the goddess within.

When she accpeted that her marriage was over, she fell in love with a woman and they began a stable partnership. Sophia studied singing and music and became politically active for peace and justice. She began to lead a variety of groups, using her voice as an instrument to help people become peaceful by opening their hearts.

SOPHIA AT A CROSSROADS

Sophia Singer stormed in, slamming the door of her own house, waking both children and scaring the cat. She kissed the kids before she heard her husband Fred shout over the booming TV, "Is that my little Sophie?"

Sophia walked into the bedroom, shut the TV off, and stood directly in front of the set, her dark eyes blazing, both fists on her hips. She said, "I am not your little Sophie. I am Sophia, your wife, and I'm demanding an explanation - now!"

"What the hell for?" Fred sat straight up in bed.

"Why didn't you tell me you had taken a military madman as a client? Why couldn't you tell me the truth: that you'd decided to publicize the campaign of a war-monger? Are you more afraid of me than the bombs or missles or...?"

Fred stared in disbelief at his normally shy wife, who only reached his chin when wearing her high heels. He had never heard her angry during their ten-year marriage.

"Sophie, either you calm down so we can talk like adults, or

Make the Circle Bigger

we're not going to talk at all," Fred glared menacingly.

"Don't threaten me, you big jerk."

Her rage caught him off guard.

Sophia threw her coat on the chair near the bed and kicked off her shoes, "I need to calm down before I say things I'll regret." She headed for the kitchen, barefooted (another first, since she always wore high-heeled slippers to compensate for her height).

Fred grabbed his robe and followed right behind saying, "That's good, Sophie, because I don't want to say anything I'll be sorry for, either." He sat, and immediately reached for a bag of cookies his mother had sent.

"How can you eat at a time like this?" Sophia asked incredulously.

"I'm nervous, that's how. I always eat when I'm nervous."

"I'd be nervous, too, if I had to sell my soul to pad my pocket."

"What is this? You about to start your period or something?"

"I am ENDING my period of playing the little lamb opposite the big bad wolf!"

"Sophie, I'm assuming you're referring to my getting Jack Ripper's campaign account. Right?"

"Right! How could you publicize a maniac like Ripper? How could you represent someone so dangerous in an election as important as this one?"

"Wait a minute!" Fred's tone was gruffer, "I don't agree with his policies, but I'm going to do a decent job for the guy, because that's my job."

"What's your job?"

"To earn enough money to keep you and the kids living in the style to which you've become accustomed!"

"So, because you want to be richer, you're willing to sacrifice your integrity, risk losing our friends, even jeopardize our lives, to get Ripper elected?"

"What's the difference between and ad man like me taking on a client he doesn't wholeheartedly support, and a lawyer representing a client he thinks may be guilty?"

"No difference at all!" Sophia said, standing like a tall person, "Selling yourself still makes you a whore."

Fred hurled the bag of cookier at Sophia, barely missing her head. "Don't you ever talk to me like that again, you bitch, or I'll..."

Sophia Singer's Communication

"Don't threaten me!" Sophia screamed, "I'm trying not to leave you."

Fred was fast and covered his shock, "If you think you can start telling me how to do my job, you can just get your little ass out the door right now. I'll be damned if I'm going to let a wife of mine make my decisions for me."

"I've started making decisions for ME. I don't have to depend on you for support. I can earn my way in the world. I have talents, too. I've stayed with you because..."

"Because you couldn't earn your way out of a paper sack! You may have delusions about being a singer, but you can't sing worth a damn. Go on, try to sing professionally, with that weak, screechy voice that nobody can stand."

Sophia stopped listening. Instead, she sat, her chin resting on her plam, and began watching Fred. She saw his tired, grey, unsmiling face and wondered what had kept her ten long years with this man she didn't like or even respect.

"He's a good father," she told herself, "a hard working provider. He's charming, when he wants to be. He's intelligent. He writes well. Sometimes he's fun."

Then she remembered how her parents used to encourage her to make the most of her marriage.

"After all," her mother would say, "he doesn't gamble, he doesn't spend his money on other women, and he's never hit you. So be grateful and act helpless."

Sophia had refused to BE helpless, though sometimes she pretended she was.

Fred was talking as if Sophia was listening.

She wasn't. She was watching his lips move and remembering...soon after their wedding, a glamorous occasion, she wore all whispy white, he was dashing, dark, complicated...too much champagne? Perhaps...

In the hotel suite, "Don't, you're going to tear my dress!"

He was too quick, too forceful.

"Women like force," he growled in her ear. He pushed her on the bed on her back and pinned her arms above her head. "You're mine, all mine!"

Too much, too soon. "No, stop! I'm not ready, I can't! Please, not like this..."

Make the Circle Bigger

Fred's dark eyes glistened...black bands of determination...power...control. He pinned her down, she screamed, he stopped.

"You're a lousy sport," he'd grumbled, rejected and angry.

They'd both cried, but he never let his tears show. It got better after that. Fred could be kind and tender, if impatient. Sometimes, he would hold her and she could explain, ever so gently, how she would like it to be. Then, if he didn't get too angry, he'd try.

She remembered suggesting they get help somewhere.

"I don't need help, you do."

She bought all the right books, but he never read them. She brought a friend home once, a therapist, but Fred was rude and rejecting. She tried different approaches and strategies, and he responded with just enough enthusiasm to keep her hoping.

Suddenly Sophia realized that not only had she stopped listening to Fred, though he kept on talking, she had begun to hear words, thoughts, and phrases that he wasn't saying. She heard the truth behind his unconvincing jargon.

When Fred said, "I know Jack Ripper's a crook, but show me a politician who isn't?" Sophia heard, "Agree with me, I need support."

"You can't tell me what I can or cannot do...," Sophia heard as, "You sound like my mother, always trying to control me."

"Men must rule. Women are dangerous because they think they can change the world...," Sophia heard as, "I have to dominate and stay in control or I'll panic. I'm afraid of you. I'd rather fight a man on a battlefield than a woman in bed."

Fred sat at the table, ranting on.

Sophia stood in the middle of the kitchen, closed her eyes and heard a melody in her head, an old children's song. She began to hum at first, and soon her body followed the melody. She swayed and twirled around the kitchen like a naughty child, escalating quickly, dancing crazy rebellious circles, singing loudly, "Who's afraid of the big bad wolf, the big bad wolf, the big bad wolf...."

Fred was stunned at first, his angry eyes unblinking as he sat and watched her antics. Then he yelled, "Sophie, stop it!"

Sophia whirled and speeded up.

"Stop that! For Christ's sake, you look like a hysterical child!"

The louder he yelled, the more frenzied she skipped and spun about on her bare feet, singing, "Who's afraid of the big bad wolf, the big bad wolf, the big bad wolf...." Louder...louder...faster....

In a flash Fred leaped at her. His hand smashed against her ear. The impact jarred her brain.

Sophia crumpled to the floor, helpless.

SOPHIA IN A GROUP

"My name is Sophia," she said softly that first night," but everyone calls me Sophie."

"What would you prefer to be called?" Lucy asked.

"I've always wanted to be called Sophia," And from that moment on, she was.

On the second day of the playshop everyone was sitting with a partner. One asked the other: what do you need? what do you want? what do you intend? The one asking the questions alternated them intuitively. The one answering said the first thing that came to mind (WAYS, *p. 30*).

"Right, wrong, stupid, clever, just answer fast!" Lucy had encouraged.

Sophia was partners with Ruby, a rather large woman with a big round, smiling face and wise brown eyes.

"What do you want?" Ruby asked.

Sophia smiled her please-don't-judge-me smile, while Ruby sat unmoved.

"What do you want?" Ruby asked again.

"I want to make the best Chinese egg rolls in the neighborhood."

"What do you want?" Ruby asked in a monotone.

"I want to be a good wife and mother," came the reply.

"What do you want?" Ruby adjusted her poncho, keeping her knowing eyes on Sophia.

"I want to be a woman, not a scared, victimized child."

"What do you need?"

"I need to be a good mother for my kids."

"What do you need?"

"I need my father's approval." A little tear formed in the farthest corner of Sophia's right eye.

Ruby was impervious, "What do you want?"

"I want to stop acting like a victim, constantly struggling to be who my father wants me to be, who my husband wants me to be, and who my children want me to be."

"What do you need?"

"I need to leave my husband."

"What do you need?"

A wave of panic floated through Sophia, "I don't know."

"What do you want?"

"I don't know."

"What do you need?" Ruby asked, loud.

"I need to know what I want."

"Good!" Ruby lost her self-control but recovered quickly, "What do you need?"

"I need to have my needs met. I need to stop lying to myself, to stop denying what I know. I've spent my whole life trying to be a good little girl." A tear slipped down her cheek but went unnoticed.

Ruby was fast, "What do you want?"

"I don't know. I don't want to be an ordinary, easy-to-forget nobody. I want to use my talents to help people, my family, myself, the planet." She ran her fingers through her short curls, pulling them back from her face.

"What do you intend?" Ruby asked at last.

"I intend to learn how to use my talents. I used to be able to sing."

"What do you intend?"

A wet, wonderful smile crept across Sophia's tear-stained face, "I intend to sing!"

On the third day, people were taking turns and, with the help of the singer and her guitar, they were singing, "I need...I want...I intend..." and filling in the blanks.

When it was Sophia's turn, she took the stick and began singing, "I need..." Her voice was too soft. People could hardly hear her.

Lucy encouraged, "Take a breath Sophia, and sing it out. You can do it."

Sophia inhaled, held on to the stick and sang softly, "I need to be free, I want to be me, I intend to be happy and..." She broke into sobs.

Someone got a mattress and put it in the center of the group.

Needing little more than the chance, Sophia lay on the mattress.

The group gathered around her.

Lucy began gently massaging her neck. As she stroked her throat, Sophia heard, "Hush Sophie, don't disturb your daddy. Be quiet. Don't make noise. Don't disturb. Don't grow up. Be my little girl."

"I'm suffocating!" Sophia gasped, clutching her throat.

Someone asked, "What is it you want to scream, Sophia? Go ahead. Let it out."

Several people helped her by gently holding her arms so she could struggle, holding her feet so she could kick.

With her head flung back and mouth opened wide, Sophia screamed a long heart-wrenching wail, "I want my voice back! I want my voice back! Give me my voice! Give me my voice! I want my VOICE!"

On the last night, the group prepared for the CELEBRATION. In just a few hours, an entire musical extravaganza had been written, rehearsed, and costumed. Comedy skits were conceived, songs created and scored, and a stage gaily decorated with everything from toilet paper to towels.

In preparation for the festival, everyone was to pick a partner and take turns painting each other's faces. Finger paints, water colors, brushes - an assortment of makeup was scattered strategically around the room.

Sophia found herself partners with Carl, an intense young man with crystal green eyes. She lay on a mattress while Carl dabbed here and there, creating just the right color, shape, and texture.

An hour flashed by. Sophia was completely relaxed and peaceful. When Carl was satisfied with his masterpiece, he held a mirror for her to see.

Sophia was delighted at being transformed into a colorful bird of undetermined origin.

Next, Carl lay in total surrender as she painted him. She lost herself in the joy of redesigning and transforming him. She was aware of her calmness, her delight.

She wished she and Fred could have so much fun. She knew they never would.

Make the Circle Bigger

Carl lay still and blissful while Sophia painted an ethereal black and blue and violet mask that so completely covered his face, he was unrecognizable.

When she finished, he laughed into the mirror. "Great!" he exclaimed, and they hugged, carefully avoiding messing-up their painted faces. Arms around one another, they pranced and played and surveyed the rest of their "family."

The scene was memorable, childlike, with everyone painted or being painted, disguised, losing all ego, losing face. In the calm, quiet, fun-filled atmosphere, people creating, enjoying. They were absorbed. Candles blazed. A never-to-be-forgotten festival was under way.

Even the worst actors and the untalented singers and dancers were fearless, swept into the spirit. Mistakes were not possible, everything was accepted. Nobody criticized. Everyone emerged a star. Even the most boring of the lot received standing ovations.

Sophia hadn't planned to perform. But with a little coaxing, especially from her buddies, Ruby and Carl, she dressed in Ruby's king-size brown shirt and Carl's old baggy pants, plus a pair of dark glasses and a rain hat. She sat timidly peering through her bird-like mask, watching the others let go.

After almost everyone had contributed some talent to the evening, Sophia was encouraged to get on the stage.

"Oh, go on," Carl prodded.

"Have some fun," Ruby coached.

Sophia stood motionless. Then, as if out of the ethers, she heard, "Who's afraid of the big bad wolf, the big bad wolf, the big bad wolf?"

She turned around slowly, her old man's garb swallowing her. She motioned to the woman who was working the lights. They had a short conference. The lights were dimmed. She was ready. She closed her eyes. Then, smiling through her bird disguise, she sang dramatically, "Who's afraid of the big bad wolf?" and threw her hat to Ruby.

"Who's afraid of the big bad wolf?" She took off the old brown shirt. The baggy pants were tossed. She stepped out of her lace panties and stood naked, her body gorgeous under the soft lights and flickering candles.

Sophia stood naked as truth. Her bird-like face was bizarre and beguiling.

Everyone was transfixed.

She bowed deep and gracefully, holding her hands together as if in prayer. She then slowly and regally straightened up and said, "I dedicate this song to the goddess in every one of us."

Then, from the depths of her soul, Sophia sang a beautiful ballad in tribute to the goddess. She sang with an electrifying quality that mesmerized and overwhelmed. Her rich, full, magnificent voice left everyone spellbound.

When Sophia finished, there was silence. Nobody applauded. Nobody moved. Some people held each other, some simply cried. But nobody would ever forget Sophia.

SOPHIA AS A LEADER

After the playshop, Sophia was strong, independent, and felt like a goddess. She gave Fred an ultimatum: either he got therapeutic help, or she'd leave him. After four months, Fred quit therapy and Sophia left home.

She and the children moved into the flat of Manuella, a beautiful woman with whom Sophia had become close friends. The more Sophia saw of the men around her, the more attractive Manuella became. They connected in a genuine selfless love that sisters share in times of need. They held each other when the pain was great, or when they rejoiced in sweet success. Ultimately, they loved themselves into lovers.

The children adjusted quickly to a consistent level of household harmony, too involved in their own new activities to wonder about the two women sharing one bed.

Sustained by her relationship with Manuella, and unafraid of being labeled or ostracized, Sophia surrendered to their inexhaustible, ever-growing love. She lived on the edge of ecstasy, sandwiched between passion and serenity. She discovered that gender is secondary to the need for compassion, understanding, and communion.

Things were perfect for a couple of years and a few playshops, until Sophia's son, Michael, began having trouble answering the questions they were being asked about their homelife. So Sophia and Manuella decided to take the boys to a weekend playshop for families.

Make the Circle Bigger

During the day parents were in sessions, while the children, led by a therapist, were in sessions of their own. In the evening the families came together to discuss, interact, and learn better ways of living together.

On the last evening, Sophia was asked to lead a SUFI CIRCLE *(p. 74)* for parents and children. She was energized. The day had gone well. Her boys were happy, they were accepting and accepted. Everyone was in the circle.

She began, "Look into each other's eyes, because if you do, you'll see stars there."

There was a flurry of delighted exclamations. Everyone saw the stars in each other's eyes.

"I'll sing the words first, then we'll sing them together. Ready?

We are the hope of the future.
We are the ones who care.
We can make a difference.
We are the ones who'll dare.
And we're growing, growing, growing, growing
Doing the best that we can.
When you see me with kindness,
I love the way I am."

The melody was lilting and rhythmic and the dance was fun. By the time it was over, everyone was exhausted and relaxed. They had laughed, sung, and played until mothers, fathers, daughters, and sons were dancing circles in peace, and Sophia knew she could lead a group.

SOPHIA'S ACTIVITIES
Sufi Circles

Sufi Circles reprogram the unconscious mind by introducing positive affirmative messages which activate the Child Ego State, where we have the power to re-decide basic life choices. Though the messages may seem naive, their power lies hidden in their childlike simplicity.

These singing messages can be used to help people get to know each other in a friendly, spontaneous, role-free way. They can be used in GATHERINGS *(p. 28)* from grade schools to universities, from churches to private parties, and can be rewritten to suit your needs. Use a popular method that suits your group, or have the most talented musicians create one on the spot.

The sufi songs offered here have been selected because they can be sung alone as musical affirmations, and danced and as well as acted-out in gatherings. Also, they involve the Tri-Energetic concepts of need-want-intend and of flexible-tolerant-curious.

When these songs are done as dances, they are always done in a circle, with partners making good eye contact. They are usually done with partners facing each other (one with the right shoulder pointing toward the center of the circle, the other with the left).

1. Sometimes I am so flexible,
Sometimes I'm tolerant,
And when I'm really curious,
My life's more interessant.
And I'm growing, growing, growing, growing,
Doing the best that I can.
When I'm flexible, tolerant, and curious,
I love the way I am.

People act-out being flexible (holding hands, bending, and swaying), being tolerant (placing their right hand on their partner's heart center, and their left hand over their partner's right hand), and being curious (cupping hands around the eyes, as if to see better). They take hands and quickly crouch to the knees at the beginning of the line "and I'm growing," and raise up to their fullest height on tip toes, with hands reaching for the sky at the end of "Doing the best that I can." On the last two lines, partners face each other, arms relaxed by their sides, knees slightly bent, feet under the shoulders and pointed straight ahead, standing in a comfortable, well-grounded posture. After partners have sung this refrain to each other, a simple way to change to a new partner is for the people with their right shoulders toward the middle of the circle to move ahead to the next person.

2. The following Sufi song and dance further helps to insure that the unconscious mind, or the psyche itself, understands the concepts of flexibility, tolerance, and curiosity.

If you're flexible, not rigid, you can bend.
If you're flexible, not rigid, you can bend.
If you're flexible, not rigid...
Please be flexible, not rigid...
If you're flexible, not rigid, you won't break!

If you're tolerant, not hateful, you can give.
If you're tolerant, not hateful, you can give.
If you're tolerant, not hateful...
Please be tolerant, not hateful...
If you're tolerant, not hateful, you can live.

If you're curious, not defended, you can know.
If you're curious, not defended, you can know.
If you're curious, not defended...
Please be curious, not defended...
If you're curious, not defended, you can grow.

The movements for "flexible" can be to take hands and sway, bending as much as possible while maintaining eye contact; "tolerant" can be the right hand on partner's heart center and the left hand over partner's right hand; "curious" can be with hands around the eyes gesturing openness and curiosity. It's fun to act out "rigid" (standing stiff), "hateful" (angry face, hands on hips), "defended" (arms crossed in front of chest), and "know" (finger pointing to head).

3. The next Sufi dance is usually done with people walking around the circle meeting new partners. It is begun with partners facing each other, as in the previous dances. Everyone holds a partner's right hand, then in rhythm with the song, goes to the next partner with the left hand, then to a new partner with the right hand, etc. The dance is a rythmic flow of meeting new partners, alternating right hand and left hand greetings, while maintaining eye contact throughout.

The flexible bend.
The tolerant give.
The curious know.
That's how we can live.
I'm flexible now.
I'm tolerant, too.

> *I'm curious to know*
> *One thing about you.*

When the music stops, at the discretion of the leader, everyone shares something personal with the person they're facing.

4. Another variation of the flexible-tolerant-curious theme offers even more physical activity and deeper personal sharing. "Sat Nam" means, "the name is truth." As you say "Sat Nam," while looking into someone's eyes, you are recognizing their inner holiness.

> *Sat Nam! Sat Nam!*
> *Let's play with flexibility.*
> *Sat Nam! Sat Nam!*
> *Please be tolerant with me.*
> *We'll be flexible and tolerant,*
> *And play with curiosity.*
> *Would you like to be friends with me?*

For deeper sharing, the last line can be changed to:
"Here's one reason to be friends with me."

When partners greet each other with the first "Sat Nam," the hands are together at the heart center in prayer position. On the second "Sat Nam," the arms are at sixty degrees, with fingers extended in an exuberant, heart-opening stretch. On "tolerant" they put right hands on their partner's heart, left hands over partner's hand. On "flexible and tolerant" they move in free form. On "play with curiosity" they turn around to the person behind them, looking curious. Everyone then turns back to their original partner, and everyone whose right shoulder is to the inside of the circle crawls between the legs of their partner to face a new partner. Looking into the new partner's eyes, sing the last line, "Here's one reason to be friends with me." Everyone then gives one reason why they would make a good friend (Pogrebin, 1987).

5. Singing your needs, wants, and intentions to a group and having the group repeat what you sang is very powerful and very beautiful. When this is done by passing a talking stick with each group member taking a turn, the focus on the one singing is even greater.

Make the Circle Bigger

Sing,

> *"I need...*
> *I want...*
> *I intend...*
>
> *She needs...*
> *She wants...*
> *She intends..."*

6. The concept of flexibility, tolerance, and curiosity can be experienced in the heart center. Deep eye contact, placing right hand on the partner's heart and left hand over the partner's right hand makes the connection even deeper. Sing,

> *"I open my heart to you*
> *And give you flexibility.*
> *I open my heart to you*
> *And give you tolerance.*
> *I open my heart to you*
> *And give you curiosity.*
> *I open my heart to you*
> *And trust you give the same to me."*

7. A beautiful, rousing group experience can be created by taking an important concept and setting it to a simple melody, so it is sung over and over as a refrain that grows in intensity. This one, for example, is a good way to begin a group session, with participants sitting in a circle or holding hands and moving together in one large circle. Sing,

> *"Make the circle bigger,*
> *Make the circle bigger.*
> *We need each other,*
> *We need each other.*
> *Make the circle bigger."*

Note: The above can be sung in as many different languages as the group can speak, adding still another dimension to our need to celebrate the universality of the human spirit. Sufi circles remind us that people everywhere have similar needs, wants, and intentions (Donahue, 1985).

CHAPTER 6

CASSANDRA THE WITCH'S INTUITION

Cassandra needed to learn how to use her psychic powers and not be afraid of them. She was alone, isolated, and unfulfilled. After discovering the power of love, she found her soulmate, released her creative sexual energy, and started a new life. She learned to accept her visions, premonitions and dreams. She began giving lectures at universities, Chanting with groups, and leading Ceremonies.

CASSANDRA AT A CROSSROADS

Cassandra was a white-haired healer who used the medicines of the mountains as her magic. An enigma, she was a living legend, though the stories told of her were as varied as the people who told them. At seventy-two, she was a young old woman with endless energy. To the people in the mountains and the little fishing village below, she was a source of wisdom and comfort - and a pain in the ass.

"Get to the point," Cassandra said briskly, not really bothering to study the beefy face of Mrs. Stumpf, the mayor's wife, who was haltingly trying to explain the "trouble" with Annie, her teen-age daughter. Cassandra had little patience with authority figures, which was why she expressly disliked the mayor without ever having met him.

Mrs. Stumpf had been reluctant to bring Annie to Cassandra anyway, but after dragging the poor girl from village doctors to big city specialists, she had succumbed to the unorthodox healing practices of Cassandra, the mountain witch.

Mrs. Stumpf, a big woman with a consistent, annoying habit of clearing her throat unnecessarily, squirmed in one of the matching wooden rockers that faced the great stone fireplace. "We've taken her to see two psychiatrists, and they both assured us that Annie would respond well to in-patient treatment, but frankly,

Make the Circle Bigger

Mayor Stumpf and I feel uneasy about leaving her in a hospital, especially since everyone knows how awful those places are."

Cassandra shuddered at the thought. Her ears got hot. The tea kettle on the wood-burning stove began to whistle. She stood, adjusted her bright red cardigan so it lay unwrinkled across her long slender waist, and offered briskly, "Can I get you some tea?"

"Thank you, yes," Mrs. Stumpf cleared her throat sufficiently to continue, "I've been quite worried about Annie for some time. She's always been a sensitive child, you know, easily offended, high-strung. But for about a month now, she's been withdrawing more and more. Now she's refusing to eat."

Cassandra, pouring the water into a pot, asked impatiently, "Why isn't Annie here so I can talk to her?"

"I don't know if she'd come."

Abruptly Cassandra put her cup on the carved bench that served as a table, "If I'm going to be of any help to Annie, I must talk directly with her," she said, wishing Mrs. Stumpf would leave.

"I'll do my best to get her here."

"If she won't come here," Cassandra said, smiling reassuringly, and indicating their visit was over, "then I'll come down to the village and visit her."

At 9 o'clock that night, Cassandra was disturbed by a loud knocking on the battered door of the cabin.

"Who in the world is that?" she mumbled to herself. She had just brushed and braided her bright white hair, and was looking forward to a hot mineral bath.

Cassandra opened the door and stared into Annie's eyes, her lashes laden with snow flakes.

Annie surveyed the room. Nothing in the compact cabin escaped her scrutiny, not the hand-loomed rug that covered the wooden floor or the open cupboards that supported the carefully labeled array of jars filled with herbs, spices, flowers, and elixirs

Satisfied that she was in the right place, Annie looked directly into Cassandra's grey-green eyes. She had a moment of hesitation and doubt, then recognition. She saw the stars in Cassandra's eyes.

At midnight, Cassandra and Annie were still rocking by the fire like long-lost sisters, reunited, joyful, and excited.

"Go on, go on," Cassandra urged, "then what happened?"

"Well, then I dreamed about a tall man with black bushy eyebrows, and the next day I was walking near the river, and there he was. I guess I was too frightened to tell anyone. But then when I started to hear the voices, when I began to hear messages about the river, I kept seeing the river poisoned, the fish belly-up and dead. All the life in the river was dead. And the fishermen, the poor fishermen! I told my mother and that's when they took me to the shrink. I knew they would think I was crazy, you know?"

Cassandra knew. After all, when she had had premonitions, heard voices, seen visions, they had locked her up in that awful place. Worse. Jesus! It had been a long time since Cassandra had allowed herself to remember.

Cassandra brought herself back. Annie didn't know she'd drifted away.

"You're going to do just fine," Cassandra smiled, "It's a great gift you've been given. We'll talk again this week. But now, it's past my bedtime."

They hugged. Annie left, unafraid. At last someone, a special someone, understood (*Krippner and Dillard, 1988*).

Cassandra couldn't sleep. She remembered. At sixteen she had been smart, blonde, some said brazen. She'd awakened from a dream, or was it? There were so many "dreams" in those days. Nobody believed her. She remembered the hospital, a nightmare of relentless needles, pills, and shocks. She had been shocked, tied, and tortured. Her arms had been crossed and bound in a straight jacket. "I'm not crazy! I'm not crazy!" she'd screamed. But nobody believed the voices she heard were real, that the images were real. She would never forget the raging electric currents of the treatment shocks.

At twenty-four she had married. A nasty man, he was. The son of a friend of her father. Still, she'd pleaded with him to stay at home one day after she'd had a terrible nightmare of an accident.

"I'm afraid there's going to be an explosion," she'd warned him.

"You're crazy!" he'd said, and was killed in the fury of the flames.

Cassandra squeezed her eyes to block the images of the past.

Finally, after hours of tossing and turning, she slept fitfully. But she dreamed of the river, the fresh blue waters black with death. She awoke with the sun, trembling with a familiar feeling of dread.

The phone rang. Her neighbor's fearful voice asked, "Have you heard about the accident? The river's been poisoned. All the fish are dead!"

CASSANDRA IN A GROUP

Cassandra only went to the playshop because Annie refused to go without her. But the lone crone gracefully accepted the ways of the young, good-naturedly learned Tri-Energetics, and tirelessly danced her way into everyone's heart. Cassandra was the star of the playshop.

It was the third morning. The group was getting ready to CHANT *(p. 91)*. They formed two circles, sitting back to back. Cassandra sat in the circle facing in, comfortable leaning against her partner.

She had never chanted before this playshop. She resented church music as much as she disliked praying. It was difficult enough to ask for anything. Praying, like begging, was out of the question.

"This mantra means victory to the power of love," Jason said enthusiastically. "Gandhi freed India with it, so let's see what it can do for us. OM SRI RAMA JAYA RAMA JAYA JAYA RAMA." "Victory to the power of love!"

OM SRI RAMA JAYA RAMA JAYA JAYA RAMA.

She found it impossible to keep her eyes closed. They kept opening and closing, like the shutter of a camera. "It's a good thing no one can see me," she thought, a little embarrassed. Then she thought, "But the only way anyone can notice my eyes being open is if their eyes are open, too," and she laughed at herself for worrying.

OM SRI RAMA JAYA RAMA JAYA JAYA RAMA.

This was different from any church service she'd ever known. There was a cheerful, lighthearted undertone to the group's harmony. It was uninhibiting to sing in this group and liberating to let her voice go. She chanted loudly and stopped thinking.

OM SRI RAMA JAYA RAMA JAYA JAYA RAMA floated around her brain, her whole body. It soothed her.

OM SRI RAMA JAYA RAMA JAYA JAYA RAMA. Cassandra soaked up the sounds. They washed and bathed her, and saturated her psyche with waves of serentiy. She lost herself in a deep and abiding peace.

On the fourth day Lucy announced, "We're going to take a JOURNEY *(p. 90)*."

Some people who had obviously taken a Journey before whooped and hollered. A few assistants helped prepare the already darkened room. Candles and incense were lit. People found mats to lie on, blankets to cover themselves.

Cassandra lay on a mat. She covered herself with a warm blanket.

"We're going to take a Journey," came Lucy's deliberately hypnotic voice, "a Journey back through time, back through our lives. It will last about an hour, so please be as comfortable as you can."

Cassandra shuffled under the blanket, adjusted her pillow, and settled down.

"My voice will guide you through your life, from the time you were just a radiant idea in the cosmos, a tiny spark of star stuff, through your infancy, adolescence, and adulthood, right until now."

Cassandra thought, "I'm so much older than everyone else, I'll probably not remember a thing."

"The music, sounds, smells, the drum, and my voice will take you deep into memories you've hidden in the very cells of the body."

Cassandra felt a little shiver run up her spine, and she pulled the blanket up to her neck and closed her eyes.

"You'll be able to see objectively the many roles you've had to play and chosen to play. If you go back to an experience you'd rather not recall, please remember that you are in control of your own Journey. If at any time you wish to come back into the present, simply sit up. One of the assistants will come and be with you."

Again, a shiver scaled up Cassandra's spine.

"Let yourself see the roles you've played opposite the signifi-

Make the Circle Bigger

cant people in your life."

Cassandra was at once excited and cautious. She thought, "No one has ever encouraged me to spend a whole hour reflecting on my past."

"Breathe. Breathe deeply, fully. That's it...long, deep, full breaths," Lucy's voice was reassuring.

Cassandra breathed deep. Her head was light, and her arms felt as though they could float up to the ceiling.

The big bass drum began to beat like a heart.

Cassandra had a magical ascent up a tree, over clouds, beyond the stars....

She heard a child-like melody, and claps of thunder rolling across stormy skies.

"There you are, a sweet and precious baby. Oh, look at the beautiful baby."

There she was, all pink and perfect. Her father, standing rigid, "Shit! I wanted a son." Her mother's tears. God, seventy-two years ago!

She heard breathing and the sounds of tinkling bells. She smelled fresh sage.

"Look at that sweet little baby face of yours. You're just starting to walk, you're so curious, wanting to explore. Who's with you? What are you doing?"

Cassandra twisted and turned, fidgeted and fumbled, but didn't see a thing.

"You're growing up. See yourself. How hard you're trying to understand, to be understood."

Cassandra saw herself a transparent girl with wispy pale hair, lace cuffs on a tan muslin gown. She dreamed in a bed she shared with a one-eyed doll, and an old blanket she used for security.

She dreamed herself walking through a misty violent crystal city. A sleek black stallion stood as if smiling. She jumped onto the animal's back and lay across him, hugging his massive neck. The great horse pranced majestically, broke into a gallop, and they were airborne. They soared upward as if racing for the moon. She was transported to the surface of a twinkling star. A group of jubilant people greeted her with outstretched arms. She walked slowly toward a sea of loving faces. She felt wanted, like a lost and weary traveler who'd found her way home. Suddenly, standing in front of her, was a duplicate of herself. The young girl, her mirror image, held her hands, "You will return to us some day. Now, return to earth as a woman who bleeds each month so the world goes on." Puff! The horse was gone. Another transparent girl with stars in her eyes and huge wings like an eagle, stood waiting to take her home.

Instead, Cassandra awakened in her dark room with her hands wet and sticky between her legs. She was twelve years old, frightened, and confused, with nobody to talk to and nobody to ask. She'd draped an old heavy coat over her delicate shoulders to shield herself from the winter's chill, and ran outside into the moonlight, searching for evidence. It came. As she squatted, a tiny drop of dark red blood fell in the new-fallen snow, spreading itself like a spider's web. Fascinated, she watched as a second drop bloomed into rose petals. Another droplet oozed onto the soft snow and she saw her own face, the stars shining in her eyes, magically reflected in the moonlight.

She'd been so innocent, so uninformed. Oh, how she'd longed for a family who understood.

Cassandra stuffed her pillow into her mouth to stifle her cries. She lay on her mat. Her fingers began to tingle, as if they'd been asleep and start to come back to life.

"Enough!" she told herself.

The combination of Lucy's trance-inducing voice and the vision of herself as an adolescent was overpowering. Cassandra escaped into sleep. Not even the beat of the drum, or the wild frenetic sounds from the cassette player could keep her awake.

When the Journey was over and practically everyone had relived painful childhood experiences, realized why they play the roles they play, and had had their catharses, the room was still. The air was filled with an intense silence, until Cassandra snored. Her snoring was so loud that it caused an outbreak of contagious laughter. People laughed until the tears rolled down their cheeks and they held their bellies and groaned. Cassandra awoke to find a room full of laughing people, and she joined right in.

Then people divided into small groups of seven, in order to more intimately share their experience of the Journey.

"How was it for you?" asked Lucy.

"I slept through it," Cassandra said matter-of-factly.

Annie stiffened, "Cassandra, you always pretend to have everything under control, but I think you're as messed up as anybody."

Cassandra was shocked. "Why? Some of us have no need to delve into our deep, dark past."

"There's so much pain and sadness in your face. Why can't you admit you need help, too?"

Lucy said, "Cassandra, we all need help, and the only way we can get it from each other is to be honest."

Cassandra was lost for words. She thought, "No one has ever cared enough about me to insist I talk about myself." She sat, looking terribly sad. She swallowed hard, clasped her icy hands to her chest, squeezed her arms together, and began shivering. Her voice was barely audible, "I'm lonely, lonely and sad. I've been lonely and isolated most all my life. I was isolated from my family because they were afraid I was a witch. I dreamed what was coming."

"I dream what's coming, does that mean I'm a witch, too?" Annie objected.

"A witch is an ordinary intuitive person," Lucy said. "People learn to use their psychic powers when they love nature, practice meditation, yoga, or use visualization."

"But I've been so afraid of my power," Cassandra said softly.

"Naturally!" Lucy said. "Everything we do is for a reward. Look how you've been rewarded for your premonitions and visions."

"I've gotten laughed at and labeled, hated and ostracized. I've been punished, locked up, and shocked." Cassandra's heart heard what her words were saying. She let go and cried.

She was laid onto her big woolen blanket and with three people holding either side, they lifted her into the air. They began to rock her. They swung the blanket gently back and forth, to and fro. They began to hum, then sing.

Sensing the intensity of the work that was happening with Cassandra, the rest of the group encircled the blanket.

It was a magical blend of human voices raised on high for the sole purpose of healing a soul. People toned their way into a symphony of sound that penetrated Cassandra's ancient walls of defense. Then, still rocking, they spontaneously began singing her name.

"I've never felt so cared for, so understood," she thought, "A witch is an ordinary woman."

Harmony, melody, healing overtones.

"When a woman is awake, she knows what's coming!"

Voices were raised in an exquisite harmony that healed.

The blanket rocked, and the group merged and became one voice, the universal voice of love. Slowly, still rocking and swaying, Cassandra was lowered to the floor. She lay with her eyes closed and tears trickling down her face. Those close enough touched her, keeping their hands on her body. Some people hummed, others still softly sang her name.

Ultimately, Cassandra opened her eyes and slowly, slowly, looked intensely at the people around her. And there it was, her dream come true, a group of people greeting her with outstretched arms. She was surrounded by a sea of loving faces. She felt wanted and accepted, like a lost and weary traveler who'd found her way home.

Lucy squeezed her big toe. "A witch is an ordinary woman who follows her intuition. She is free to dream a dream and create the winds of change to make it happen. You seem to have conjured a rather large family for yourself."

Annie stroked Cassandra's wonderful white hair that now lay loose and tousled about the blanket, "I love you, Cassandra. You're my favorite witch in the world."

Cassandra smiled, wiped her teary eyes and said, "This witch knows the healing power of love." And she knew she would never be lonely again.

CASSANDRA AS A LEADER

Nearly a year after the playshop, Cassandra wrote Lucy.

Dear Friend,

There was a time when I wondered if there was life after menopause. Now I'm wondering if there was life before it. I have met a man of wit and wisdom and we have recognized the stars in each other's eyes!

I will be seventy-three this month, and I'm quite aware of what society thinks of people my age succumbing to the arrows of eros. I've managed to remain unimpressed by the dictates of our

Make the Circle Bigger

narrow-minded culture, and consequently have allowed myself a great adventure.

I know that from time to time I have connected with the universal mind. I have seen things as they actually are, without the filtering system of the ego to disguise the lies. But this is the first time I have experienced lucidity simultaneously with another living being.

Manfred has lifted my spirits, and raised me to a level of clarity that enables me to see (clairvoyantly) insights and perceptions about just about everything. We play as children do, exploring virgin territories of hearts and minds, and using the power of love to beguile and enchant. And when his love empowers me, I know that a goddess is a woman who knows the power of love, and I know that a witch is a woman who knows she's a goddess. So, like all good witches, I conjure and concoct, and when he wants a song, I am a canary; when he needs to rest, I disappear; and when he dreams of a young girl, I become one! Oh, it's lovely to be reaping the harvest in the twilight!

I've been so inspired that I phoned an acquaintance at the university and offered to lecture on the medicinal properties of the local plants. It's the first time the establishment has treated me with respect, not to mention tolerance and curiosity!

Last month at the full moon, several of the playshop family came to my cabin to chant and have a CEREMONY (*p. 89*). I suggested that while we chanted we could release something we no longer wanted in our lives by symbolically throwing it into the fire.

Everyone took responsibility for the Fire Ceremony. Someone gathered wood and someone brought musical instruments. We gathered close enough to the water's edge to hear the gentle rush of the river.

We were circled round the fire, holding hands. Someone thanked the spirits of nature and we sang a beautiful song for the Earth, and the silver sliver of moon seemed to notice and glow in gratitude.

We got silent.

After we had ample time to contemplate what we wanted to throw away, we began to chant ONG NAMO GURU DEV NAMO to call upon the inner teacher. The vibrations were powerful indeed.

People approached the fire one at a time, focusing on what was no longer wanted. Each walked slowly and silently around the fire three times, while the group chanted.

After everyone had taken a turn, I realized I didn't know what I wanted to get rid of. I had no thoughts at all, but I began walking around the fire, Chanting with the others. I remember feeling the warmth of the flames. By the third time around, I knew what I needed to give up: my fear of my psychic powers. When I returned to the circle, Manfred took my hand and I realized I was no longer afraid!

See you at the next playshop.

Love, Cassandra

CASSANDRA'S ACTIVITIES

Ceremonies

Ceremonies acknowledge and celebrate something. Whether a spontaneous happening or a formal ritual, Ceremonies bring people together. Don't be intimidated by formal rituals. Ceremonies don't have to be formal, costly, conventional, or inconvenient (Starhawk, 1979). If your intentions are clean and clear, you'll get what you want. When we're free to explore and unafraid of mistakes, Ceremonies help life become a Celebration.

1. A FIRE CEREMONY can be as simple as finding a fireplace and consciously acknowledging something. If there's no fireplace available, consider using a candle in the middle of an old washtub, or weather permitting, build a small fire outdoors.

Gather two or more people. Take a few moments to become centered and calm. Breathing together helps. Chant or simply sit in silence until everyone is present and attentive.

Write down something you no longer need, don't want, and intend to get rid of. For example, if someone has been abusing a drug that's damaging their health, they may write, "nicotine."

Then, one at a time, let each person consciously throw their "unwanteds" into the fire, with the intention: I RELEASE THIS NEGATIVE INFLUENCE FOR THE HIGHEST GOOD OF ALL, while the group supports the process by either chanting, singing, or simply acknowledging what's happening.

Simple, easy-to-arrange fire Ceremonies often bring meaningful and lasting changes. Note: Children love fire. Don't deprive them of its ritual healing benefits.

2. A HEALING CEREMONY is not weird or hocus-pocus, and you don't have to be a psychic, mystic, or shaman to have one.

Invite some friends over. Sit in a circle. Light a few candles (four is best—one for each element and direction). Let someone in the group who needs healing lie in the middle of the circle. Chant her or his name lovingly, or chant **OM SRI RAMA JAYA RAMA JAYA JAYA RAMA** (for healing through the power of love). You may chant whatever pleases you, or don't chant - sing soflty. Let each person in the circle visualize (see) the one to be healed, as healthy! See her smiling, healthy, and peaceful.

If appropriate, let some of the group touch the person gently. It's healing just to feel someone's hands on your forehead, or holding the heels of your feet. This often creates a space for a release of tension in the form of a good cry, which (like laughing and singing) is an excellent way to feel better.

Healing Ceremonies can be powerful, if you let them. Remember, they are not used to "cure" people. Rather, they provide an atmosphere in which the one being healed can relax deeply enough to stimulate their immune system.

3. COMMITMENT CEREMONIES are wonderful ways to publicly acknowledge an intention in your life. A commitment is a pledge of allegiance with heart. It stirs your honor system and reminds you of who you are. If you can keep your commitments, you can trust yourself.

If you want to make a public commitment, have a Commitment Ceremony. For example, two women found their biggest fear was of being alone in life. They decided to commit to being friends forever. They invited some people to a Ceremony. They sat in a circle, and everyone offered a few words about friendship. Then the two women pledged their friendship, an unconditional love, and acceptance of each other, forever. Their promise gave them each a feeling of safety, plus the security that the supportive community that witnessed the Ceremony would help them keep their commitments.

Journeys

Journeys are trance-like voyages into altered states of consciousness. They offer relief from ordinary mundane thinking, and fortunately don't require drugs.

In playshops, we often take Journeys back through our lives with the clear intention of releasing old traumas. But at home, in a small group, you can Journey together with some friends for any noble intention. You can Journey into the future, or Journey to find a symbol for protection, or to find a spiritual guide. Just enjoying good music together in a group can be a powerful Journey *(Winter, 1985)*. Don't underestimate your ability or talent to act as a guide for other people's Journeys. Journeys are available on cassettes and in books, or create your own.

After the group (or person) is relaxed and lying down comfortably, encourage them to breathe deep, reminding them that the deeper and slower they breathe, the further they will go.

Remember to speak slowly and clearly. A little drama helps when delivering emotional material.

Allow about an hour for a Journey, and always remember to give people enough time to return to their ordinary consciousness after any trance-like experience. Encourage them to stretch the body, inhale and yawn, rub the palms of the hands together and the soles of the feet together, then slowly open the eyes and come back to the here and now.

Chanting

Chanting out loud (especially in a group) with a full breath and a full heart brings quiet focus to the mind. Chanting mantras is especially effective for correcting negative beliefs, thoughts, and feelings that limit us. Mantras are sound patterns that create specific thoughts, feelings, and physical effects that transform our unmanifest potential into energy in action.

Mental focus at the brow center, while correctly intoning a mantra, vibrates nerve centers in the palate and cranium, and produces specific electro-chemical changes in the nervous system. Intensity of devotion is the key that brings results.

Chant the mantra of your choice one hundred eight times each day for forty days. This many repetitions locks the mantra's vibration in your physical body, so that it is not lost in the ups and downs of life. Note: Sorry, but if you miss a day you have to start over. Not to worry, you have nothing to lose but your anxiety.

If you're not Chanting with a group, try Chanting AT LEAST the first 36 repetitions at full volume and vibrate the sound in the head and chest. If the mind stays restless, continue out loud (many times this is necessary in our chaotic culture). If you are becoming quiet, the second 36 repetitions can be Chanted silently, moving the lips with no sound, and the last 36 can be Chanted mentally *(Keshavadas, 1980)*.

Chanting mantras awakens the Sound of the Spirit in the heart center, sending affirmative messages directly into the nervous system. The sound is the meaning; mantras mean what they say.

Mantras must be heard and felt for their vibrations to be transmitted. If no teacher is around, recordings are essential *(Keshavadas, 1985)*. Although no book can give you the experience of chanting, what follows are some Himlayan mantras, which are valuable tools for quieting the mind, and for bringing you into harmony with the divine.

1. TO AWAKEN INTUITION -
    ONG NAMO GURU DEV NAMO

This mantra brings you in contact with the pure white light within. It's great to tune-in to higher consciousness by chanting three times: before yoga, before Chanting another mantra, before taking an exam, or anytime.

Meaning "I call on the teacher within," this Mantra aligns individual intelligence with infinite consciousness.

This mantra can be Chanted as a bhajan (devotional song) in the form,

ONG NAMO GURU DEV NAMO
ONG NAMO GURU DEV NAMO
NAMO NAMO GURU DEV NAMO
NAMO NAMO GURU DEV NAMO

Find the melody that opens your heart to the wisdom and protection of your inner teacher.

2. FOR VICTORY TO THE POWER OF LOVE -
    OM SRI RAMA
    JAYA RAMA
    JAYA JAYA RAMA

This is the mantra for overcoming lust or anger, and for nonviolent conflict resolution.

RAMA is an incarnation of the highest lord, Vishnu, a perfect balance of masculine solar energy *(RA)* and feminine lunar energy *(MA)*, and as such is an incarnation of love. SRI means power and JAYA means victory.

Rama Mantra, or Taraka Mantra, is a raft that takes the sincere aspirant across the ocean of misery, in the eternal rescue of the individual soul by the power of love.

This mantra is Chanted by millions of people every day with hundreds of different melodies and rhythms. It's slightly irregular sonic pattern is central to the healing, liberating effect it transmits. For group meditation and healing, the last line can be repeated twice *(JAYA JAYA RAMA)*, or the entire mantra can be chanted *(OM SRI RAM JAY RAM JAY JAY RAM)*. These variations help adapt the mantra's transformative irregularities to western groups.

3. FOR PROTECTION BY THE POWER OF LOVE -
    KODANDA RAMA PAHI
    KODANDA RAMA
    PATABIRAMA PAHI
    PATABIRAMA

This bhajan celebrates the power of love that brings protection. Rama's great bow is called KODANDA. With it, the godly king Rama overcame unthinkable adversaries to rescue his beloved soulmate, Sita. Chanting the sound RAMA drives away evil influences, cleanses the area of negativity, and brings peace.

CHAPTER 7

LUCY LEADER'S COSMIC CONNECTION

Lucy made a cosmic connection when she transcended her personal separateness, and experienced a unity with life itself. She trusted her intuition, followed her inner guidance, and dropped her personal defenses. In the safety of a group, she let go of the role of group leader, faced her fear of a future catastrophe, and let herself be helped. By surrendering to her absolute truth, she empowered people to recognize their individual divinity. She inspired others to make the cosmic connection, and she awakened a sense of belonging to a global community.

LUCY AT A CROSSROADS

Nobody knew that on the day she was to begin an Inner Peace Playshop, Lucy Leader was a nervous wreck.

The morning began innocently enough. She and her husband, Jason, had spent the night at the old farmhouse where the playshop was being held. She'd slept soundly until a ray of sun found its way through the crack in the shade.

"Good morning, sunshine goddess," Jason whisper-kissed into her naked shoulder.

Lucy snuggled close to him, completely forgetting that she always remained silent the day a playshop began, and whispered sleepily, "God, I love you."

"You are a ripe and juicy apple hanging from the tree of life, just waiting to be picked and eaten. Do you know how loved you are?"

Lucy thought, "Sometimes," remembering she was supposed to be in SILENCE (*p. 47*). She was grateful she didn't have to answer. She was grateful that her children were grown and living their own lives, and loved her. She was grateful that her life's work brought her happiness and purpose. And she was grateful for Jason, who she knew was a gift from God.

Make the Circle Bigger

After an enjoyable silent breakfast, Lucy, looking out the second-story farmhouse window, thought, "I'm going for a walk before it rains." She kissed Jason's cheek, indicating she was leaving, and headed for the woods.

Walking through the orchard, Lucy remembered Jason telling her she was a ripe and juicy apple. She smiled wryly as she saw the trees looked sick, and walked into the woods thinking, "The tree of life is struggling to stay alive."

Lucy walked faster. She was strong and well-conditioned, but her heart was more than pounding, it was aching.

Then, she had a flash: "Therapy means movement; movement means motion; motion equals emotion." She ran deeper into the woods, thinking, "If I keep this up, I'll either be euphoric or dead!" She laughed.

Suddenly Lucy stopped and stood still. Cautiously and gingerly, barely turning her head, she began to look around. Finally, she saw what she'd been trying not to see. There they were! The dead and dying trees (*Hofmann, 1988*). Some had already fallen, some were greyish-green, and some looked as if they'd been sprayed a strangely ominous yellow.

Images flooded Lucy's psyche. The trees looked like painfully naked, helpless children.

"What is this? I need to quiet down, to get peaceful. I can't keep thinking about this."

She trudged up the steep mountain road, breaking her silence by mumbling to herself, then abruptly sat down and began to write.

> *For Sale: One Damaged Planet*
> *Planet Earth, priced fair.*
> *Poisoned water, food, and air.*
> *Trees still standing, here and there.*
> *Oceans, rivers need repair.*
> *If interested in living space*
> *Help them quick - it's a disgrace!*
> *Inhabitants are mad and greedy,*
> *Kill their own, starve the needy.*
> *Still, a few are conscious beings*
> *Making changes, seeing things.*

> *If interested, apply to Earth.*
> *State what you think the planet's worth.*

As she finished, the sun began to play tag with some dark clouds. The clouds were winning. Lucy felt weak and shaky and the wind was blowing cold. In a flash, she was overcome with an unfamiliar, unnatural silence, the sound of abandonment. She felt drained and dry. The air was depleted. The woods were deserted and lifeless, devoid of spirit.

Lucy headed back to the house and Jason. By the time she opened the door to their room, Lucy was ashen. Jason took one look at her and, knowing full well she was in silence, asked, "What's wrong?"

"The weather has turned unseasonably freezing, I have a rock in my shoe, I'm about to start my period, I'm tired, my head hurts, and there is going to be a catastrophe in the neighborhood soon."

"You're having a premonition?" Jason was steady, "Can you say more?"

"The spirits have left the woods. The woods have lost their spirit."

"You mean it's something more than the trees are dead and it feels spooky?"

"The spirits of the woods have gone and what's coming is anybody's guess..." and Lucy began to shake with icy chills.

"Here, get under some warm blankets," Jason said, helping her under the covers. "Let me hold you until you stop shaking."

"This is ridiculous," Lucy said through chattering teeth, "I'm supposed to show people how to get peaceful? What a joke."

"You have several hours before the playshop starts, Sweetheart. You'll be fine."

Almost as if she hadn't heard him, Lucy said, "We have to give people a crash course in cooperation because people around here are going to really need each other."

Jason was beginning to feel more uneasy.

"What is it?" he asked, sounding calm, covering his concern.

"People can only use what they have learned to use."

"What?" Jason asked, not understanding what she meant.

"We cannot use what we have not learned to use!" *(Shah, 1967)* She was emphatic.

Make the Circle Bigger

"Okay, I believe you. But what are talking about?"

"I'm not sure, but I think we're going to find out."

An hour later, after a hot bath and a hot cup of tea, Lucy was feeling almost normal. Jason left to arrange the group room. Minutes later, Cassandra knocked on the door.

"I hope it's alright to intrude on you privacy," Cassandra said, hugging Lucy, "but I'm in such terrible shape at the moment, I'm tempted to leave before we start."

"What's wrong?" Lucy asked.

"I have a strong sense that something terrible is going to happen - here!"

Lucy took Cassandra's icy hands in hers, looked directly into her eyes, and said, "I know!"

LUCY IN A GROUP

Lucy sat in the circle holding a remarkable carved shamanic TALKING STICK (*p.* 29). "This is an ordinary stick," she said, smiling, a twinkle in her eye, "There's nothing magical about it!"

A few people laughed knowingly.

"This ordinary wooden stick can, however, convert mundane thoughts and desires into meaningful miracles, if you let it."

Some people giggled.

"Just hold the stick with both hands with your right hand on top, take a deep breath, and say your name and what you want from this playshop."

Lucy listened carefully as people one by one passed the stick and gave their reasons for being there. When it was her turn, Lucy took a big breath, and said, "I want us to have five fun-filled days of joy and laughter. I want us to learn to use our talents, knowledge, and skills wisely. Maybe we can't escape our personal pain and problems, but we can transcend them."

The evening went fast and soon the group was relaxed and ready for bed.

Lucy intended to explain the schedule for the next day but her heart was full of the pain of premonition.

"We have a chance here to learn how to cooperate during this playshop", she said lightly. "Those of you who live in this area will need to know how to help one another, because there's going to be a major problem here."

There was a ripple of murmuring, whispers, and questions.

Sophia asked nervously, "Should I go home? My children are with a baby sitter."

Lucy said immediately, "No, I don't think anything's going to happen until after the playshop," and she looked at Cassandra for confirmation.

Cassandra, holding Manfred's hand, nodded in agreement.

"Is there anything we can do to prevent something from happening here?" Richard asked.

"Great question," Lucy said, brightening, "Anybody care to respond?"

Sophia said quickly, "We all know that our world is standing on edge..."

Harriet interrupted her with a good-natured laugh, "I just want to be sure I get to enjoy myself before we go over that edge."

"It doesn't matter THAT we're standing on the edge of the world. What matters is HOW we're standing on the edge of the world," Rita said sincerely.

"It's the quality, not quantity, of life we're working for," Sophia said optimistically.

Lucy, scanning the circle said, "I accept there's nothing I can do to now to prevent some future event from happening here. Do you agree?"

Agreement from the group was clear.

"Let's not stand on the edge of the world alone. We need each other," Harry offered.

"In that case," Lucy said happily, "we need to Celebrate our need for each other." She smiled, stood up, and said jovially, "Let's play! Let's make a SUFI CIRCLE (*p. 74*) and sing and dance. Let's CELEBRATE (*p. 30*) that we need each other."

People were exhausted. Most of the group had had a long journey that day.

"We'll all sleep better if we play for just a few minutes before we go to bed," Lucy encouraged.

Everyone held hands, made a big circle, and began singing,

"MAKE THE CIRCLE BIGGER
MAKE THE CIRCLE BIGGER
WE NEED EACH OTHER

WE NEED EACH OTHER
MAKE THE CIRCLE BIGGER"

The energy in the room instantly changed. The atmosphere became light-hearted and fun as people played like children. Holding hands, they ran quickly into the center at once, then they backed up very slowly. They laughed and danced and looked into each other's eyes as they played. People trusted one another. They felt safe.

They sang loud, with full voices, and they sang softly, with compassion and intensity. They sang with opened hearts and they sang in five different languages.

They sang and danced and Celebrated friendship and love. They Celebrated belonging to a family of individuals who would help each other in times of need.

They Celebrated getting the message. They Celebrated life!

There was nothing else to do.

Everyone went to bed feeling peaceful.

The next three days were intense, exhausting, and exhilarating. People's lives had changed. Everyone was feeling exuberant. Nobody thought much about Lucy's premonition.

A Ceremony to Celebrate inner peace had been planned for the third night of the five-day playshop. Lucy announced at dinner that she needed to step out of her role as group leader because she was tired and needed peace herself.

The room looked beautiful for the CEREMONY (*p. 89*). Candles flickered in the center of a lovely, peaceful circle.

The ceremony began with chanting the word PEACE in several languages. Each person was to take a deep breath and sing the word that the person on their left had just sung. Jason began with SHANTI, then sang FRIEDEN, SHALOM, SALAM, PEACE, PAIX....

Lucy, sitting on Jason's right, was carefully following him, singing with one full breath the word he'd just sung.

After thirty minutes of the ceremony, the variety of sounds and tones was exquisite. People looked serene and calm.

Lucy was deep in trance when, without any conscious change in her intentions, she suddenly sang out, "Help."

Sophia, sitting next to Lucy, was shocked. She didn't know whether to sing "Help" or another word for peace. She realized she needed to chant something, or the person on her right would not know what to do.

Sophia sang, "Help," as gently as she could manage.

On her next turn, Lucy sang, "Earth."

Again Sophia didn't know what to do. She sang, "Earth," as lyrically as possible.

Jason knew something was up with Lucy. He looked at her.

Her eyes were closed, her spine was straight. Then she sang out, "PLEASE!" in a voice that was not hers. She continued to wait her turn, then instead of repeating what Jason had sung, she kept alternating "Help", "Earth," and "Please." Finally, she stopped waiting for her turn and put the words together, "Help Earth Please. Help Earth Please." Louder and louder, over and over, she sang intensely aand soulfully, "HELP EARTH PLEASE!"

Everyone stopped chanting. Nobody said a word. Except for Lucy's voice, which kept escalating in volume and intensity, the room was still.

Then Lucy screamed, "WAKE UP! WE NEED EACH OTHER. WE CANNOT USE WHAT WE HAVE NOT LEARNED HOW TO USE." Her screams turned to sobs.

Jason helped her into the center of the circle. Somebody laid a blanket down to cushion her, and the group gathered around.

Some people were shocked that Lucy had gone into her pain with total abandon. But everyone helped comfort her. Harriet held her first, and Lucy cried like a baby in her arms. Everyone gave something, by stroking, holding, and giving loving energy.

Jason let the others enjoy giving to her, knowing it was seldom she allowed herself to step out of the role of group leader.

Finally, after Lucy was relaxed and herself again, the group decided to continue the ceremony, and she felt peaceful at last.

If Lucy intended to give the group a MESSAGE (*p. 103*), she succeeded. Everyone received a different message, and each interpreted the message according to the level of consciousness in which it was perceived.

In the closing circle, people were telling what they did in the world and what they had to offer each other.

"I can help you with your dieting, exercise, and prejudices against fat people," Harriet offered in her inimitable way.

Make the Circle Bigger

Harry spoke about the gatherings he and Anna hosted.

Rita offered her support group for those interested in breaking a smoking addiction.

Richard suggested people come to him for therapy, whether they could afford it or not.

Sophia offered her singing and sufi dance groups, and encouraged people to participate with her in some cause for peace and justice.

Cassandra offered her mountain cabin for full moon gatherings and weekly chanting groups.

A supportive community had become a reality. Neighbors who had scarcely known each other had become friends. Prejudices had disappeared. Old feuds had evaporated.

Despite her premonition that people would need each other as never before, Lucy's hope for the future returned as people offered their knowledge and skills, their talents, friendship, and love. She felt optimistic as she saw how beautiful people looked in their natural loving state.

Five days after the playshop ended,
a nuclear power plant exploded in Chernobyl, Russia.
Soon the area where the playshop had been held
was saturated with radioactivity.

LUCY AS A LEADER

Once there was a woman who had a recurring dream. She'd see herself endlessly awakening people, saying, "We need each other. We cannot use what we have not learned to use."
Not understanding the message, she traveled seeking knowledge, wisdom, and truth, until at last she stopped searching and forgot about the dream.

The woman had a large family. She taught them all she knew of life - how to inspire people to be flexible, tolerant, and curious; how to discover the needs, wants, and intentions of the soma, psyche, and soul. She learned that peace was possible in the magic of a healing circle.

One day an explosion of materials man had not yet learned to use poisoned a continent and the woman understood her dream:

*The world can be destroyed by the greed of those
who dare to use what they have not learned to use.
The world can be saved by those dreamers of peace
who know the power of love and how to use it.*

LUCY'S ACTIVITIES
Messages That Matter

Most of us are so saturated with irrelevant and erroneous Messages that we can't think for ourselves *(Williams, 1978)*. Most of us are in psychic shock, and vulnerable to thought control *(Wilson, 1987)*.

Intelligence is a matter of how well we can think for ourselves. Intelligence is limited by consciousness. Higher consciousness is accessible in Silence. Meditation, walking in nature, yoga, chanting, sitting still, communing with someone, and gazing into a candle's flame or at the embers of a fire give us a chance to hear the truth.

We need to be silent long enough to hear Messages that matter. We need each other, and we need leaders who are flexible, tolerant, and curious enough to get that Message.

> *Seven people standing on the edge of the world heard a message, "You can use only what you have learned to use."*
> *They each understood the message according to their own level of consciousness.*
> *A suicidal housewife thought the message meant she needed to learn how to survive.*
> *A handsome philanderer realized he needed to learn that sex was sacred.*
> *A lawyer saw that she needed to learn the power of good will.*
> *A disheartened student felt he needed to learn to love.*
> *A talented young mother heard her inner voice crying and knew she needed to learn to sing.*
> *A mountain witch knew she needed to trust her intuitions.*
> *A group leader, knowing the edge of the world is a terrible place to be standing when you're all alone, brought them together in a circle to learn to use the power of love to get what they needed.*

The Seven Stretches

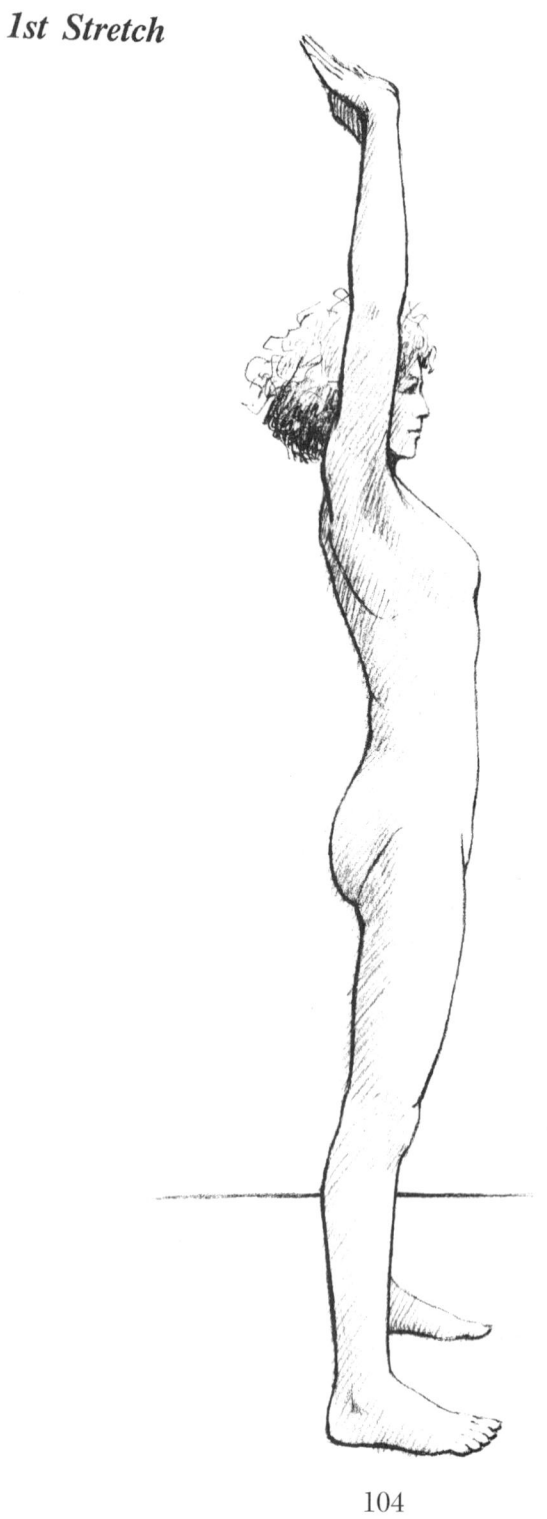

1st Stretch

Seven Stretches

2nd Stretch

Make the Circle Bigger

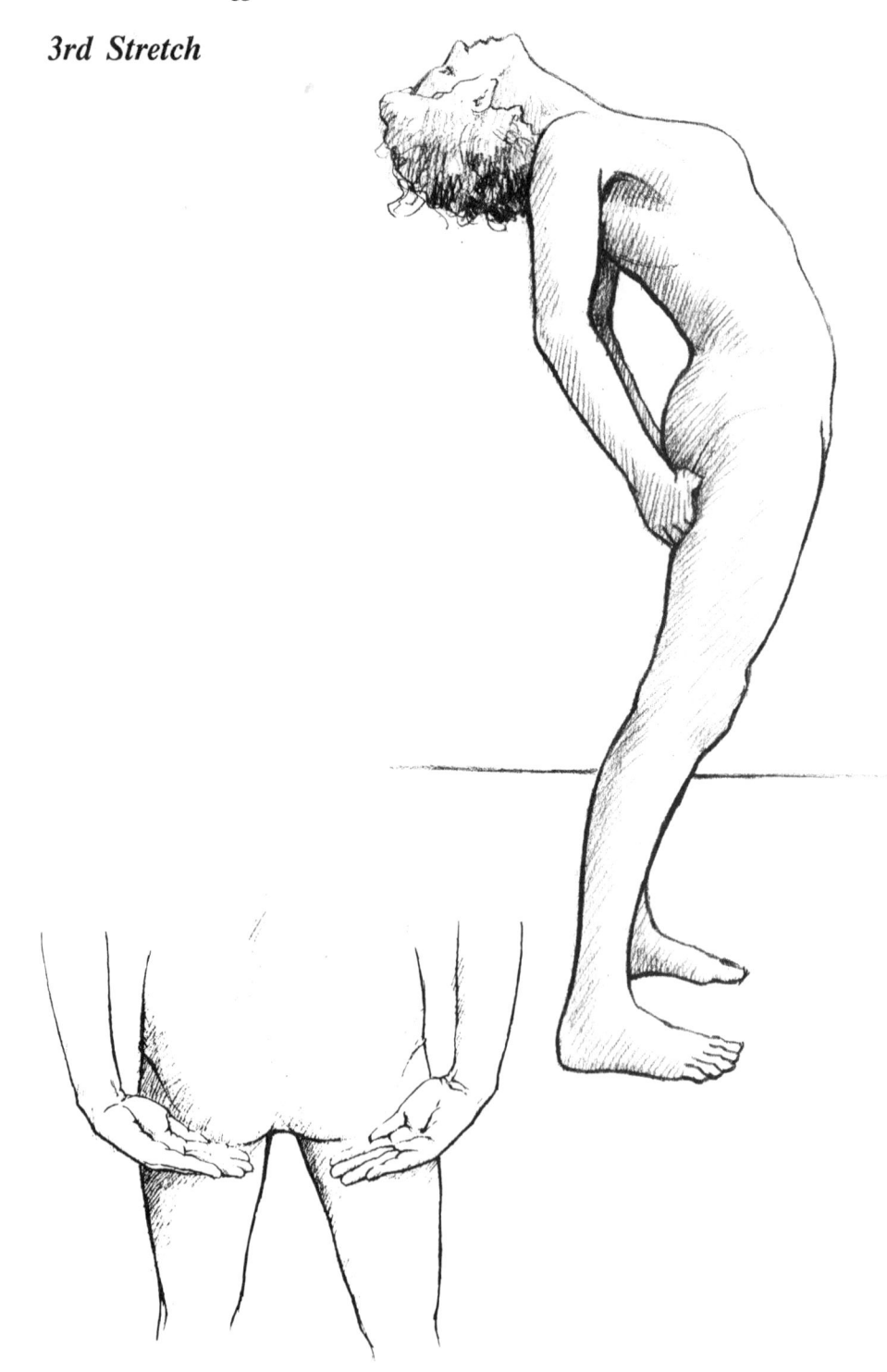

3rd Stretch

Seven Stretches

4th Stretch

Make the Circle Bigger

5th Stretch

Seven Stretches

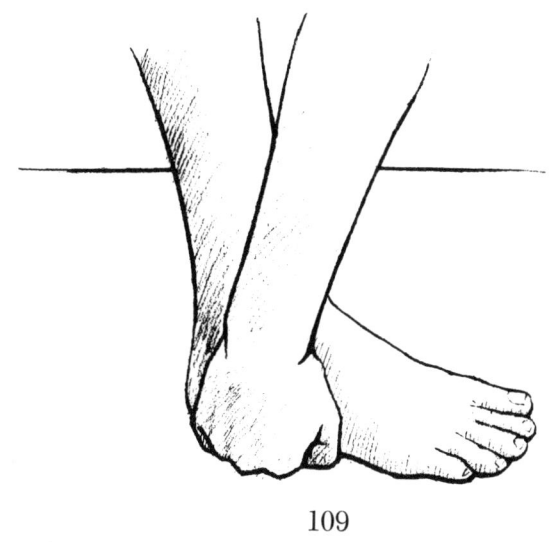

6th Stretch

Make the Circle Bigger

7th Stretch

BIBLIOGRAPHY

BOOKS THAT INSPIRE

Barnaby, Frank. *The Gaia Peace Atlas*. Pan Books, 1988.
Berne, Eric. *Games People Play*. Ballantine Books, 1978.
Donahue, Phil. *The Human Animal*. New York: Simon & Schuster, 1985.
Gould, Roger L. *Transformations*. New York: Simon and Schuster, 1979.
Grigg, Ray. *The Tao of Being*. Atlanta, GA: Humanics New Age, 1989.
Grigg, Ray. *The Tao of Relationships*. Atlanta, GA: Humanics New Age, 1988.
Hamel, Peter M. *Through Music to the Self: How to Appreciate and Experience Music Anew*. Compton, 1976.
Heider, John. *The Tao of Leadership*. Atlanta, GA: Humanics New Age, 1985.
Hoffman, Abbie. *Steal This Urine Test: Fighting Drug Hysteria in America*. Penguin Books, 1987.
Hofmann, Albert. *Insight Outlook*. Atlanta, GA: Humanics New Age, 1989.
Kahn, Si. *Organizing: A Guide for Grassroots Leaders*. McGraw-Hill, 1981.
Keshavadas, Satguru Sant. *Healing Techniques of the Holy East*. 1901 Fruitland Ave. Oakland, CA 94601: Temple of Cosmic Religion, 1980.
Krippner, Stanley and Dillard, Joseph. *Dreamworking*. Buffalo, NY: Bearly, Ltd., 1988.
Leonard, George. *Walking on the Edge of the World: A Journey of Discovery Through the Sixties and Beyond*. Houghton-Mifflin, 1988.
Lessing, Doris. *Shikasta: Re-colonized Planets*. Vintage, 1981.
Ley, Adano. *Basic Five Stretches*. Houston, TX: 1987.
Macy, Joanne. *Despair and Personal Power in the Nuclear Age*. New Society, 1983.
Messing, Bob. *The Tao of Management*. Atlanta, GA: Humanics New Age, 1989.

Moore, Rickie. *A Goddess in My Shoes: Seven Steps to Peace.* Atlanta, GA: Humanics New Age, 1988.

Myers, Norman. (Ed). *The Gaia Atlas of Planet Management.* Pan Books, 1985.

Namikoshi, Toru. *Shiatsu Stretching.* Japan Publications, 1985.

Pogrebin, Letty Cottin. *Among Friends: Who We Like, Why We Like Them, and What We Do With Them.* McGraw-Hill, 1987.

Rifkin, Jeremy. *Entropy: A New World View.* Bantam, 1981.

Rosenberg, Jack Lee and Rand, Marjorie. *Body, Self & Soul: Sustaining Integration.* Atlanta, GA: Humanics New Age, 1985.

Rowan, John. *The Horned God.* London and New York: Routledge & Kegan Paul, 1987.

Shah, Idries. *Tales of the Derivshes.* Dutton, 1967.

Smith, Fritz Frederick. *Inner Bridges.* Atlanta, GA: Humanics New Age, 1986.

Starhawk. *The Spiral Dance: A Rebirth of the Ancient Religion of the Great Goddess.* Harper & Row, 1979.

Stockmyer, John and Williams, Robert. *Life Trek: The Odyssey of Adult Development.* Atlanta, GA: Humanics New Age, 1987.

Trebach, Arnold S. *The Great Drug War.* MacMillan, 1987.

Ventura, Michael. *Shadow Dancing In the USA.* Tarcher, 1985.

Walker, Barbar G. *The Crone: Woman of Age, Wisdom and Power.* Harper & Row, 1985.

Williams, Paul. *Das Energi.* Warner, 1978.

Wilson, Robert Anton. *The New Inquisition.* Falcon, 1987.

Yoganda, Paramahansa. *Autobiography of a Yogi.* Self-Realization Fellowship, 1981.

MUSIC THAT INSPIRES

Freedman, Cindy. *Song Spirit*. P.O. Box 66566, Houston, TX 77006, 1985.

Freedman, Cindy. *Gift of Love*. P.O. Box 66566, Houston, TX 77006, 1987.

Grigg, Ray. *The Tao of Relationships*. P.O. Box 7447, Atlanta, GA. 30309. Humanics New Age Audio, 1990.

Heider, John. *The Tao of Leadership*. P.O. Box 7447, Atlanta, GA. 30309. Humanics New Age Audio, 1988.

Keshavadas, Satguru Sant. *Cosmic Healing Mantras*. 1901 Fruitland Ave. Oakland, CA 94601: Temple of Cosmic Religion, 1985.

Ley, Adano. *Prismer of Love*. Vol. 1,2,3. Houston, TX: 1987.

Moore, Rickie. *A Goddess In My Shoes*. P.O. Box 7447, Atlanta, GA. 30309. Humanics New Age Audio, 1990.

Perkins, Michael. *Island Fantasies*. P.O. Box 7447, Atlanta, GA. 30309. Humanics New Age Audio, 1990.

Streisand, Barbara. *One Voice*. CBS Records, 1986.

Winter Consort, Paul. *Concert For The Earth*. Litchfield, CT: Living Music Records, 1985.

Winter Consort, Paul. *Earthbeat*. Litchfield, CT: Living Music Records, 1987.

Make the Circle Bigger

ORGANIZATIONS THAT INSPIRE

ENVIRONNET ° Greenpeace 24-hour computer network for environmental protection alerts. 1 (415) 861-6503

GREENPEACE ° Leaders in environmental protection.
1638 R Street NW, Washington, DC 20009 ° 1 (202) 995-8787

PACIFICA NEWS ° Highly accurate with minimal hype.
National Public Radio, Washington, DC ° 1 (202) 783-1620

SIERRA CLUB ° Dedicated to the glory of nature.
730 Polk St. San Francisco, CA 94109 ° 1 (415) 776-2211

UNITARIAN UNIVERSALIST ASSOCIATION ° Social action and religious philosophy for a better world.
25 Beacon St., Boston, MA 02108 ° 1 (617) 742-2100